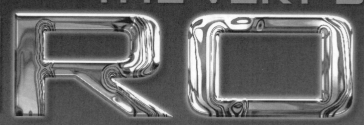

THE VERY BEST OF ROCK

EASY GUITAR WITH NOTES & TAB

ISBN 0-634-07003-7

HAL•LEONARD® CORPORATION

7777 W. BLUEMOUND RD. P.O. BOX 13819 MILWAUKEE, WI 53213

Visit Hal Leonard Online at
www.halleonard.com

Guitar Notation Legend

Guitar Music can be notated three different ways: on a *musical staff*, in *tablature*, and in *rhythm slashes*.

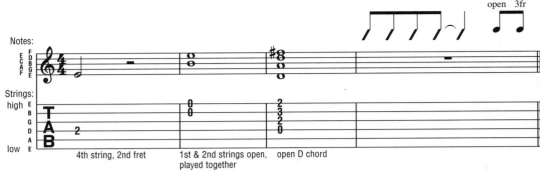

RHYTHM SLASHES are written above the staff. Strum chords in the rhythm indicated. Use the chord diagrams found at the top of the first page of the transcription for the appropriate chord voicings. Round noteheads indicate single notes.

THE MUSICAL STAFF shows pitches and rhythms and is divided by bar lines into measures. Pitches are named after the first seven letters of the alphabet.

TABLATURE graphically represents the guitar fingerboard. Each horizontal line represents a string, and each number represents a fret.

4th string, 2nd fret   1st & 2nd strings open, played together   open D chord

HALF-STEP BEND: Strike the note and bend up 1/2 step.

WHOLE-STEP BEND: Strike the note and bend up one step.

GRACE NOTE BEND: Strike the note and immediately bend up as indicated.

SLIGHT (MICROTONE) BEND: Strike the note and bend up 1/4 step.

BEND AND RELEASE: Strike the note and bend up as indicated, then release back to the original note. Only the first note is struck.

PRE-BEND: Bend the note as indicated, then strike it.

VIBRATO: The string is vibrated by rapidly bending and releasing the note with the fretting hand.

WIDE VIBRATO: The pitch is varied to a greater degree by vibrating with the fretting hand.

HAMMER-ON: Strike the first (lower) note with one finger, then sound the higher note (on the same string) with another finger by fretting it without picking.

PULL-OFF: Place both fingers on the notes to be sounded. Strike the first note and without picking, pull the finger off to sound the second (lower) note.

LEGATO SLIDE: Strike the first note and then slide the same fret-hand finger up or down to the second note. The second note is not struck.

SHIFT SLIDE: Same as legato slide, except the second note is struck.

TRILL: Very rapidly alternate between the notes indicated by continuously hammering on and pulling off.

TAPPING: Hammer ("tap") the fret indicated with the pick-hand index or middle finger and pull off to the note fretted by the fret hand.

NATURAL HARMONIC: Strike the note while the fret-hand lightly touches the string directly over the fret indicated.

PINCH HARMONIC: The note is fretted normally and a harmonic is produced by adding the edge of the thumb or the tip of the index finger of the pick hand to the normal pick attack.

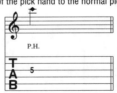

PICK SCRAPE: The edge of the pick is rubbed down (or up) the string, producing a scratchy sound.

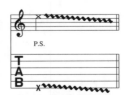

MUFFLED STRINGS: A percussive sound is produced by laying the fret hand across the string(s) without depressing, and striking them with the pick hand.

PALM MUTING: The note is partially muted by the pick hand lightly touching the string(s) just before the bridge.

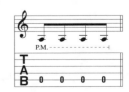

RAKE: Drag the pick across the strings indicated with a single motion.

TREMOLO PICKING: The note is picked as rapidly and continuously as possible.

VIBRATO BAR DIVE AND RETURN: The pitch of the note or chord is dropped a specified number of steps (in rhythm) then returned to the original pitch.

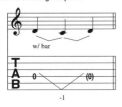

VIBRATO BAR SCOOP: Depress the bar just before striking the note, then quickly release the bar.

VIBRATO BAR DIP: Strike the note and then immediately drop a specified number of steps, then release back to the original pitch.

STRUM AND PICK PATTERNS

This chart contains the suggested strum and pick patterns that are referred to by number at the beginning of each song in this book. The symbols ⊓ and ∨ in the strum patterns refer to down and up strokes, respectively. The letters in the pick patterns indicate which right-hand fingers plays which strings.

p = thumb
i = index finger
m = middle finger
a = ring finger

For example; Pick Pattern 2
is played: thumb - index - middle - ring

Strum Patterns

Pick Patterns

You can use the 3/4 Strum or Pick Patterns in songs written in compound meter (6/8, 9/8, 12/8, etc.). For example, you can accompany a song in 6/8 by playing the 3/4 pattern twice in each measure. The 4/4 Strum and Pick Patterns can be used for songs written in cut time (¢) by doubling the note time values in the patterns. Each pattern would therefore last two measures in cut time.

Authority Song

Words and Music by John Mellencamp

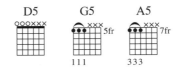

Drop D tuning:
(low to high) D-A-D-G-B-E

Strum Pattern: 1, 2

Intro

Moderately

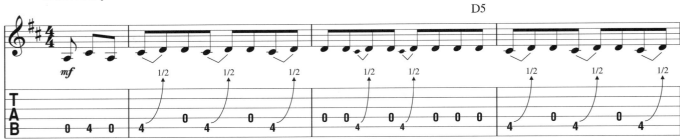

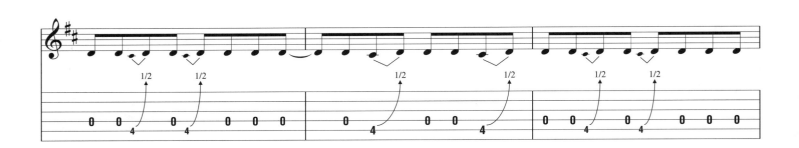

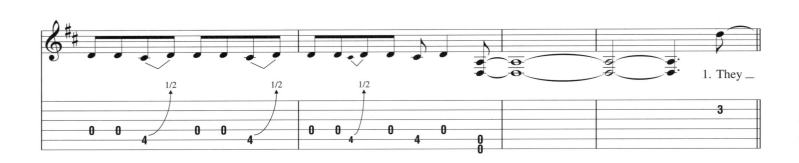

Verse

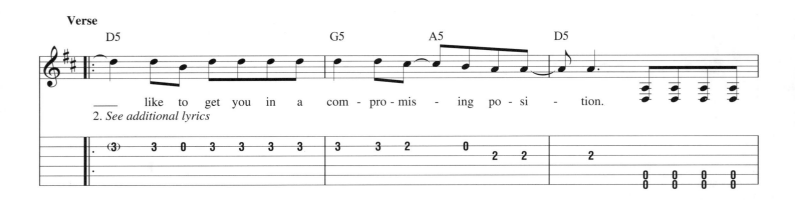

_____ like to get you in a com-pro-mis-ing po-si- tion.

2. See additional lyrics

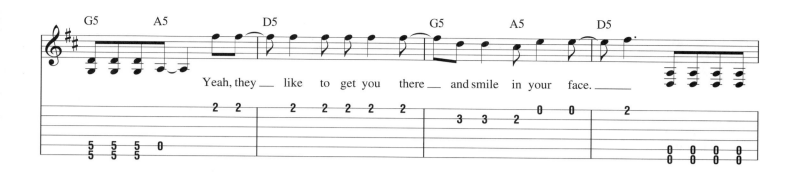

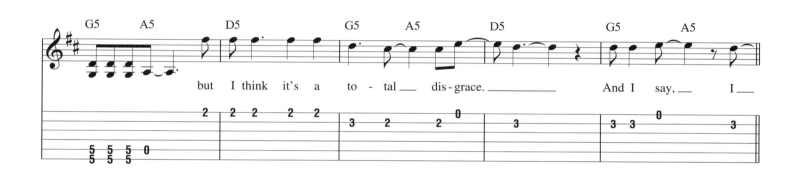

𝄋 Chorus

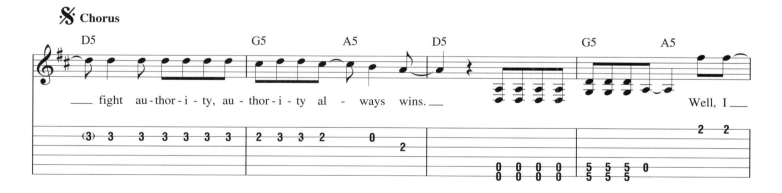

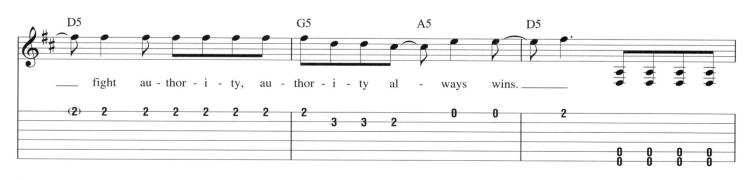

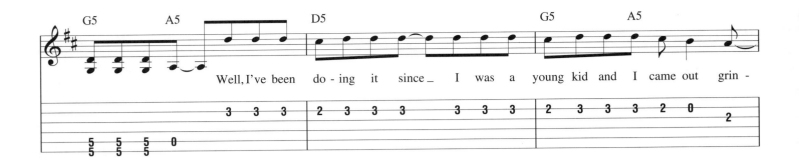

Well, I've been do-ing it since _ I was a young kid and I came out grin-

-ning. Well, I _____ fight au-thor-i-ty, au-thor-i-ty al - ways wins. _

Interlude

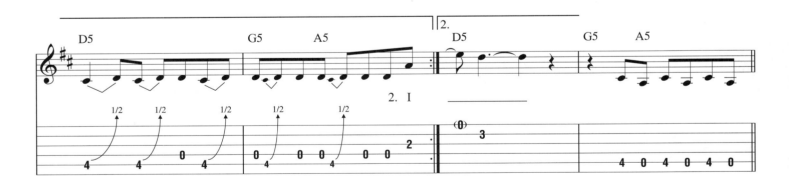

2. I _____

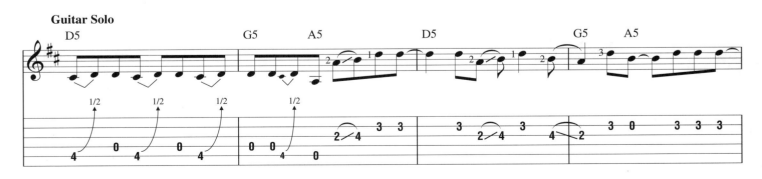

Guitar Solo

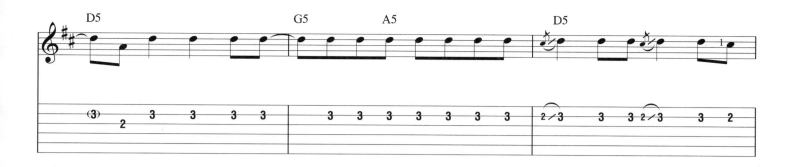

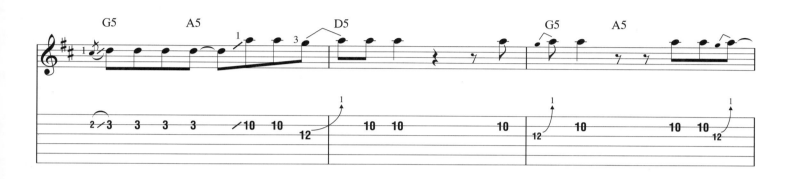

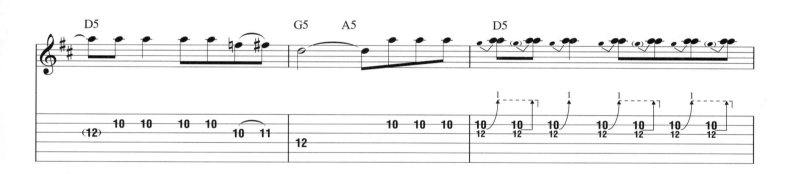

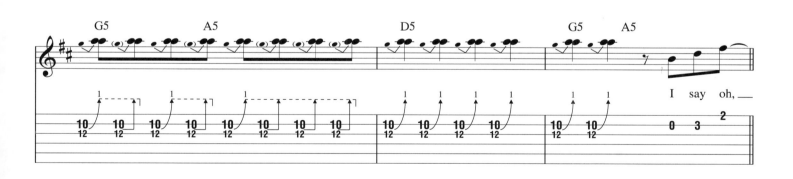

Interlude

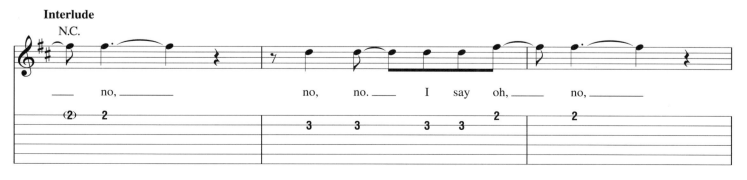

no, no. I say oh, no, no, no, no.

Chorus

N.C.

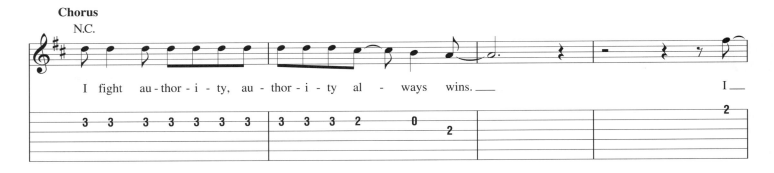

I fight au - thor - i - ty, au - thor - i - ty al - ways wins. I

fight au - thor - i - ty, au - thor - i - ty al - ways wins. *Spoken: Kick it in.* I've been

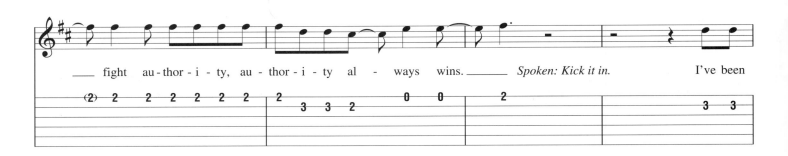

do - ing it since I was a young kid and I've come out grin - ning. Well, I

D.S. and fade

fight au - thor - i - ty, au - thor - i - ty al - ways wins. Well, I

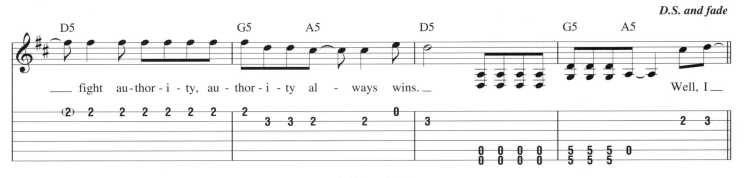

Additional Lyrics

2. I call up my preacher, I say, "Give me strength for round five."
He said, "You don't need no strength, you need to grow up son."
I said, "Growing up leads to growing old and then to dying,
Ooh, and dying to me don't sound like all that much fun."
And so I say...

Day Tripper

Words and Music by John Lennon and Paul McCartney

Strum Pattern: 2, 5
Pick Pattern: 4

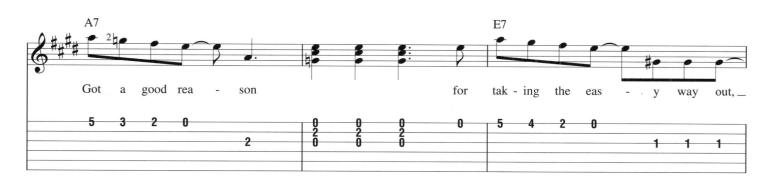

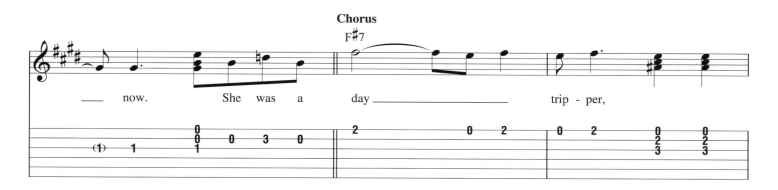

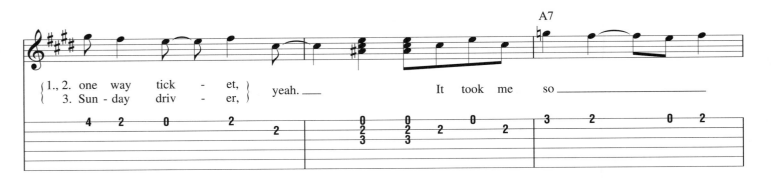

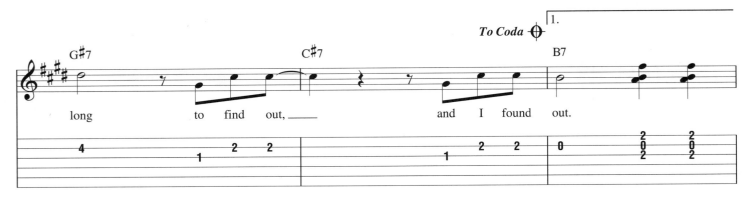

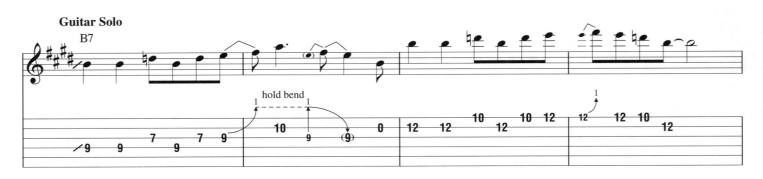

10

Breakdown

⊕ Coda

Outro

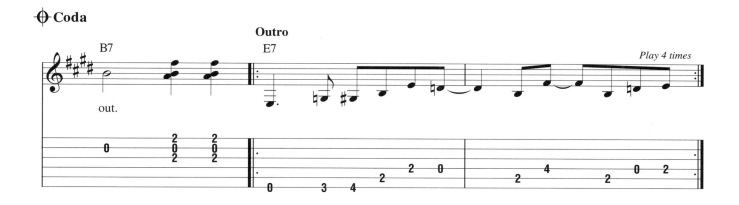

Play 4 times

out.

Repeat and fade

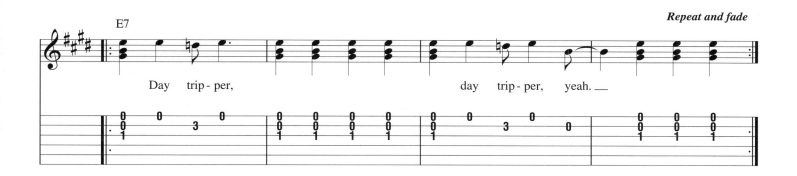

Day trip-per, day trip-per, yeah. ___

Additional Lyrics

2. She's a big teaser.
   She took me half the way there.
   She's a big teaser.
   She took me half the way there, now.

3. Tried to please her.
   She only played one night stands.
   Tried to please her.
   She only played one night stands, now.

Barracuda

Words and Music by Roger Fisher, Nancy Wilson, Ann Wilson and Michael Derosier

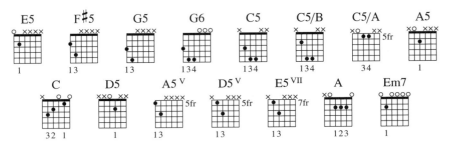

Strum Pattern: 1, 2

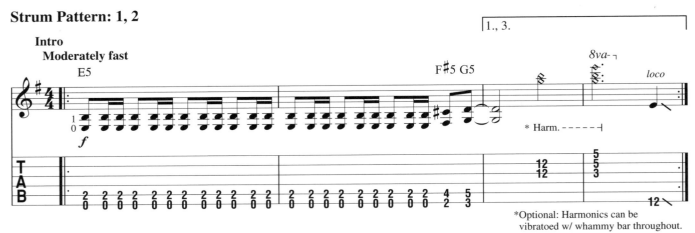

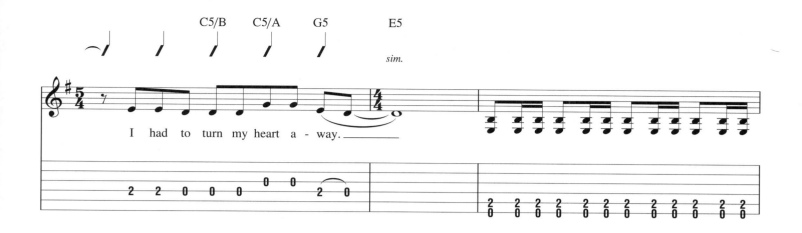

I had to turn my heart a - way.

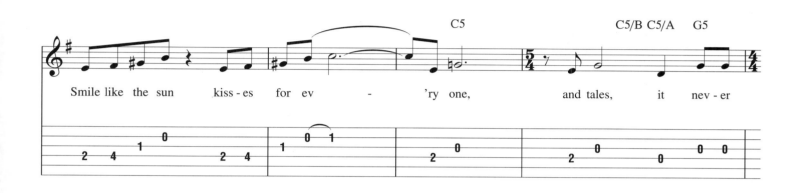

Smile like the sun kiss - es for ev - 'ry one, and tales, it nev - er

Chorus

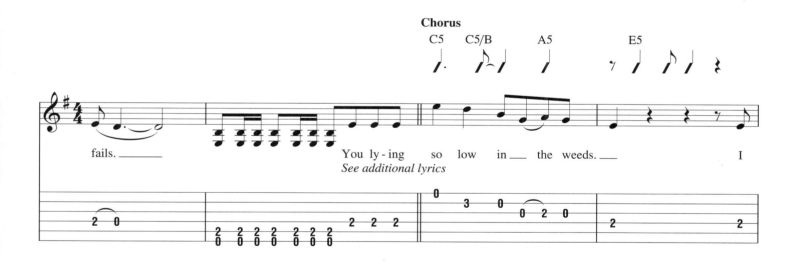

fails. _____ You ly - ing so low in ___ the weeds. _____ I

See additional lyrics

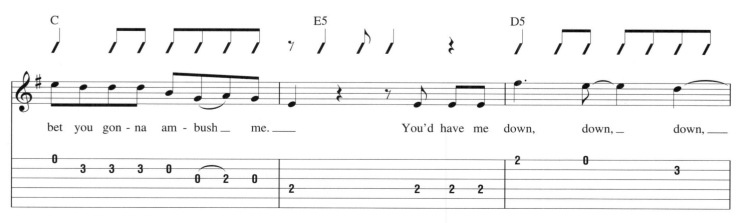

bet you gon - na am - bush ___ me. _____ You'd have me down, down, ___ down, ___

Bridge

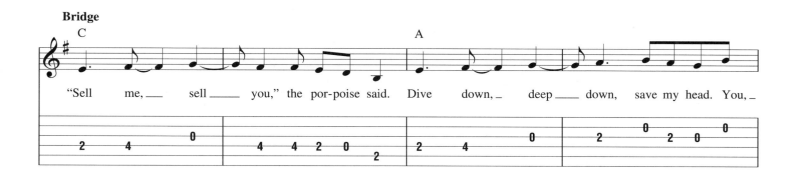

"Sell me, ___ sell ___ you," the por-poise said. Dive down, _ deep ___ down, save my head. You, _

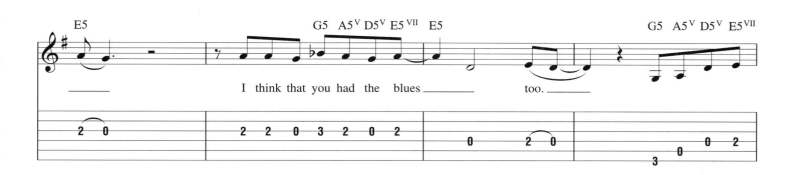

___ ___ I think that you had the blues ___ too. ___

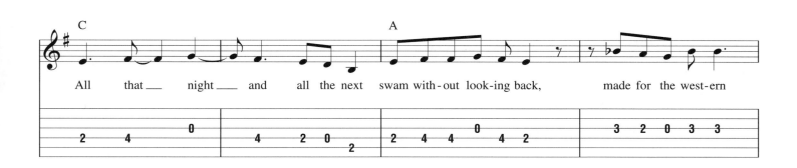

All that ___ night ___ and all the next swam with-out look-ing back, made for the west-ern

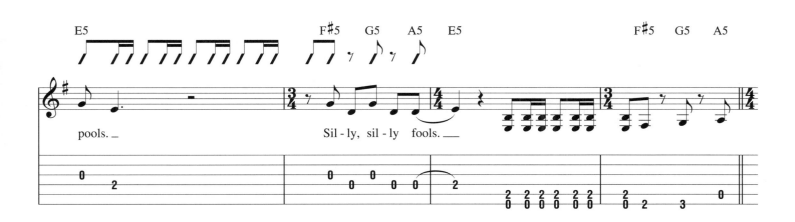

pools. _ Sil - ly, sil - ly fools. _

Guitar Solo

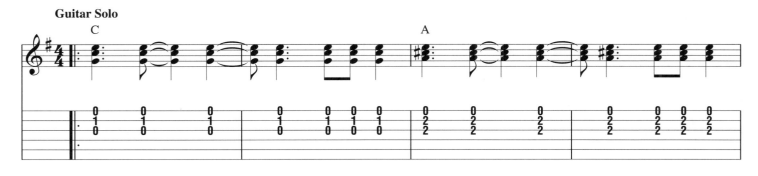

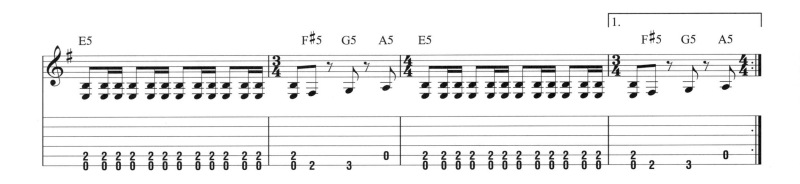

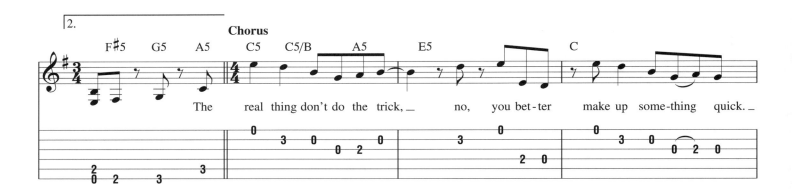

Outro

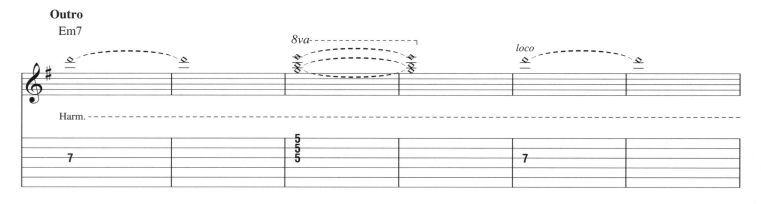

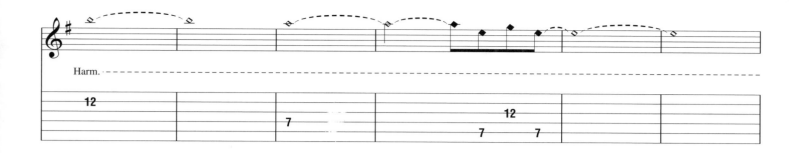

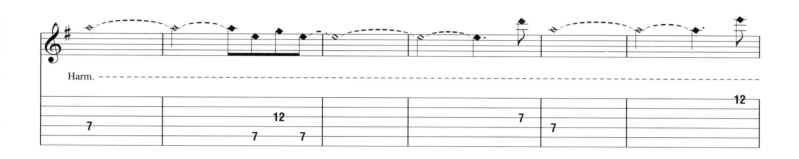

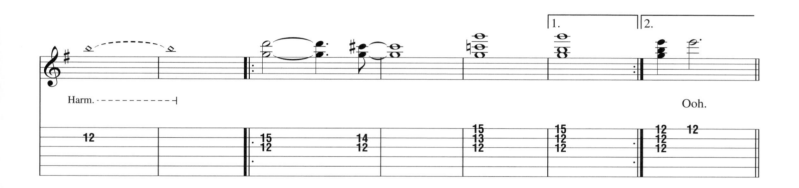

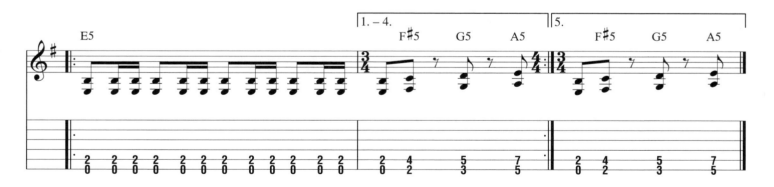

Additional Lyrics

2. Back over time we were all trying for free,
You met the porpoise and me. Uh huh.
No right, no wrong; selling a song,
A name. Whisper games.

Chorus And if the real thing don't do the trick,
You better make up something quick.
You gonna burn, burn, burn, burn,
Burn it to the wick.

Behind Blue Eyes

Words and Music by Pete Townshend

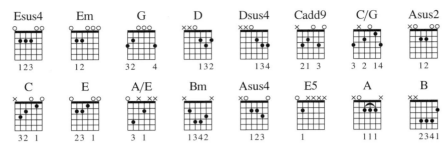

Strum Pattern: 3
Pick Pattern: 2

Intro
Moderately

1. No - one knows _ what it's like _ to be the bad man, _ to be the
2. No - one knows _ what it's like _ to feel these feel - ings _ like I

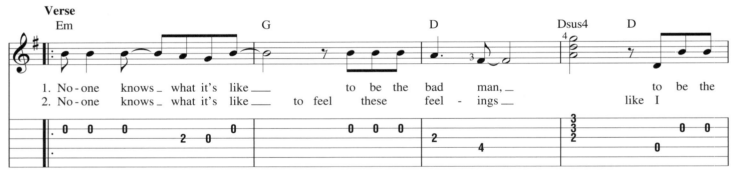

sad man _ be - hind _ blue eyes.
do, and I blame _ you.

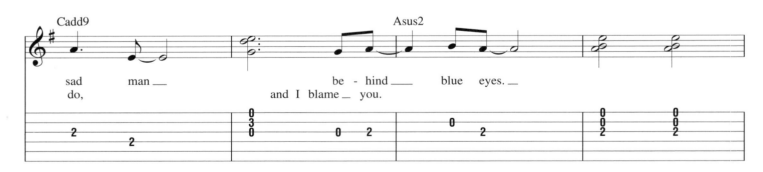

No - one knows what it's like _ to be hat - ed, _ to be
No - one bites _ back as hard _ on their an - ger, none of my

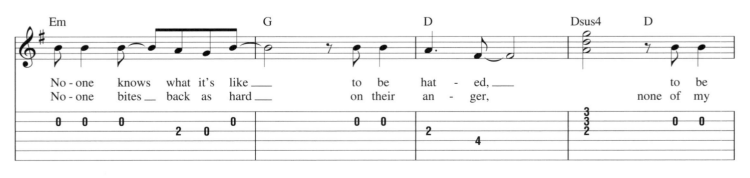

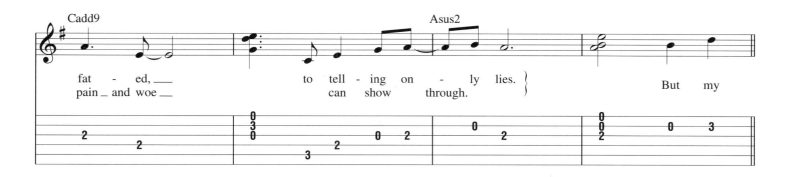

fat - ed, ___ to tell - ing on - ly lies.
pain _ and woe __ can show through.

But my

Chorus

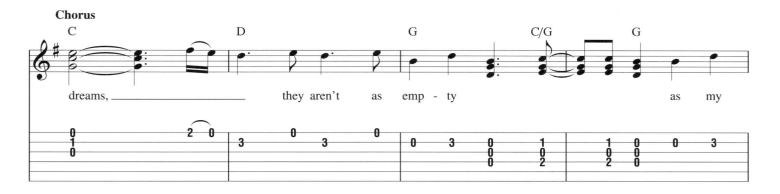

dreams, _____ they aren't as emp - ty as my

con - science seems ____ to be. ___ I have hours _____

_ on - ly lone - ly. ___ My love is ven - geance

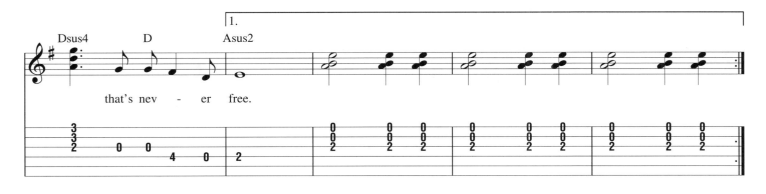

that's nev - er free.

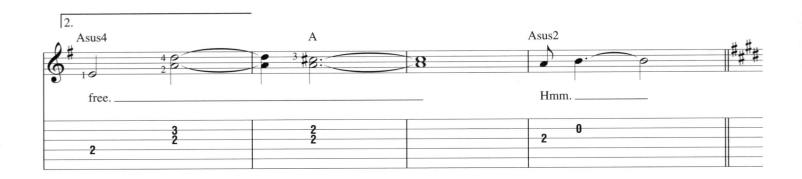

free. Hmm.

Interlude
Double-time feel

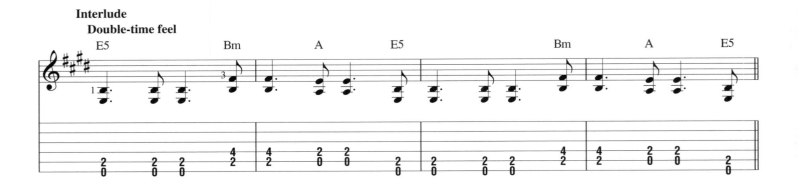

Verse

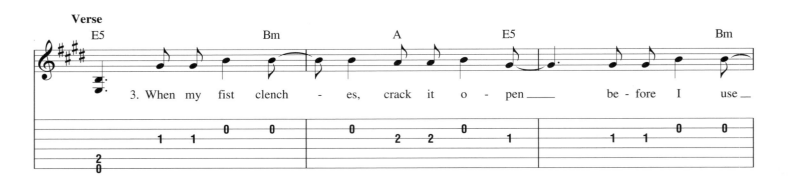

3. When my fist clench - es, crack it o - pen _____ be - fore I use _____

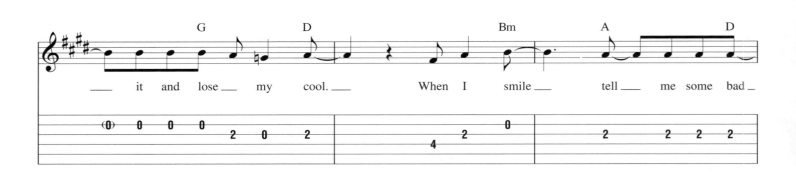

_____ it and lose _____ my cool. _____ When I smile _____ tell _____ me some bad _____

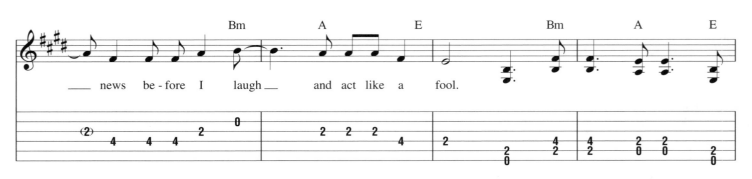

_____ news be - fore I laugh _____ and act like a fool.

20

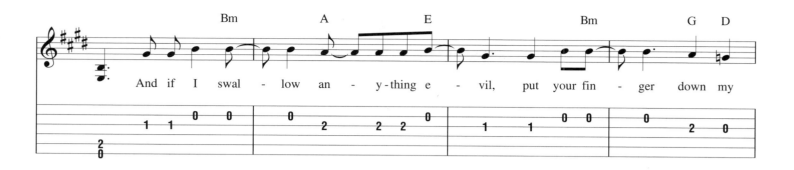

And if I swal - low an - y-thing e - vil, put your fin - ger down my

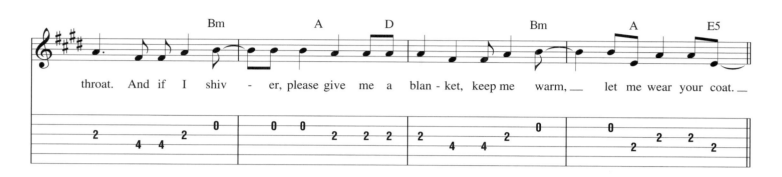

throat. And if I shiv - er, please give me a blan - ket, keep me warm, __ let me wear your coat. __

Interlude

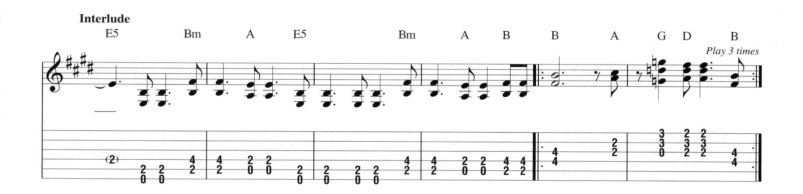

Play 3 times

Outro

No-one knows __ what it's like __ to be the bad man, __

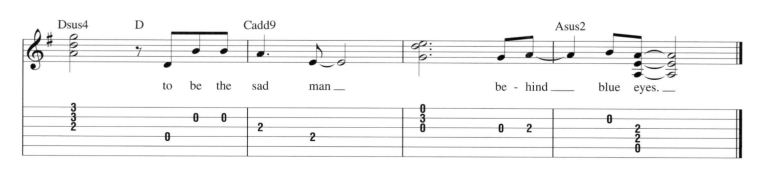

to be the sad man __ be - hind __ blue eyes. __

Hey Joe

Words and Music by Billy Roberts

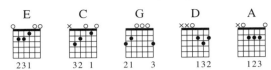

Strum Pattern: 4
Pick Pattern: 2

Intro
Moderately slow Rock

Verse

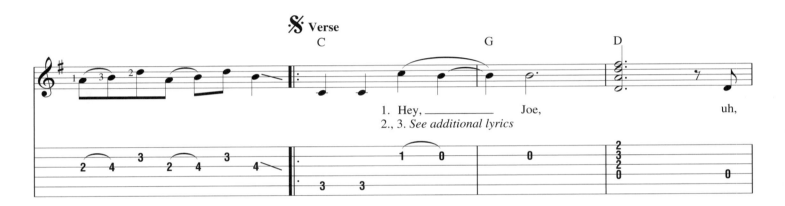

1. Hey, _____ Joe, uh,
2., 3. *See additional lyrics*

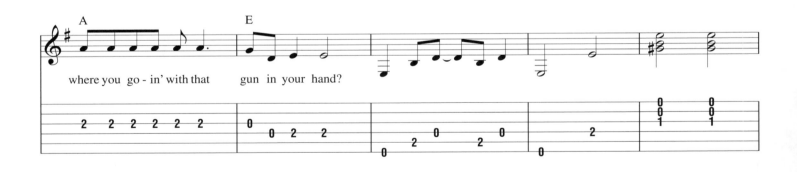

where you go - in' with that gun in your hand?

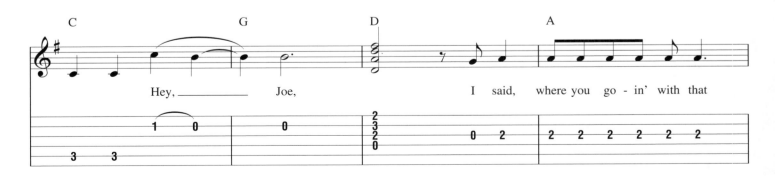

Hey, _____ Joe, I said, where you go - in' with that

gun in your hand? Al - right.

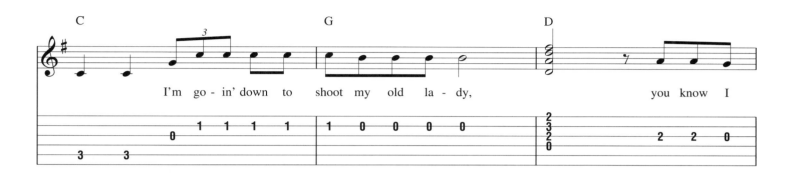

I'm go - in' down to shoot my old la - dy, you know I

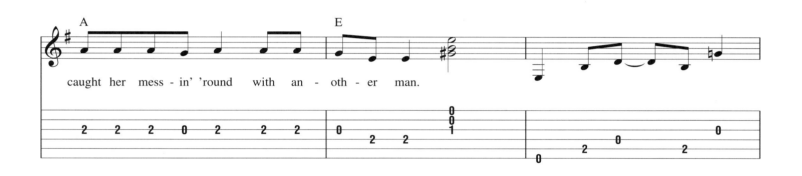

caught her mess - in' 'round with an - oth - er man.

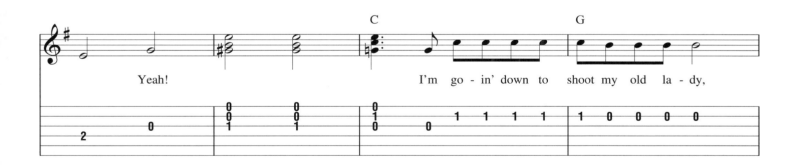

Yeah! I'm go - in' down to shoot my old la - dy,

To Coda ⊕

1.

you know I caught her mess - in' 'round with an - oth - er man.

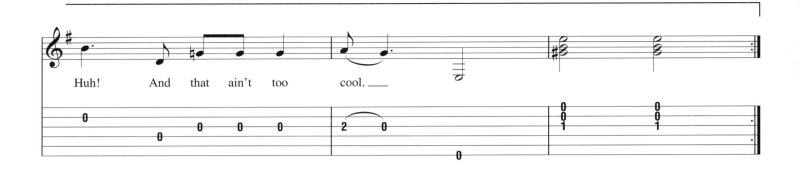

Huh! And that ain't too cool. ___

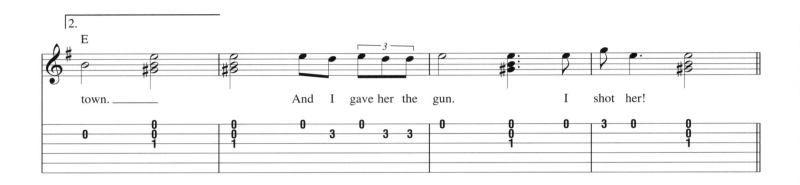

2.

town. ___ And I gave her the gun. I shot her!

Guitar Solo

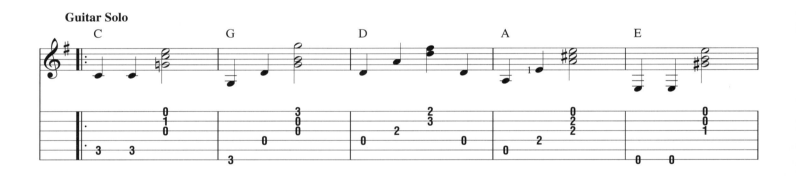

C G D A E

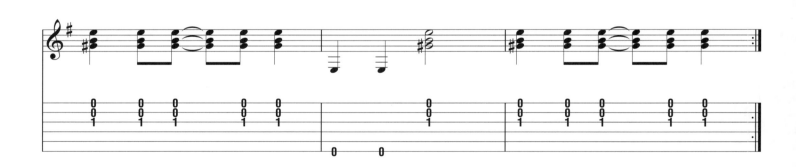

Interlude

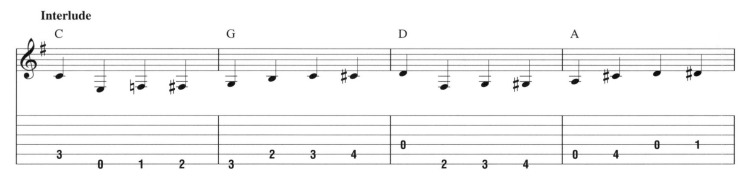

C G D A

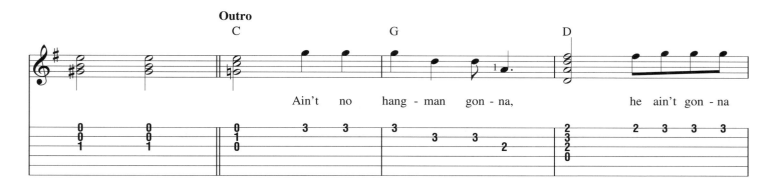

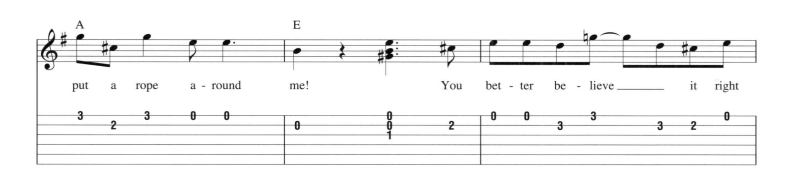

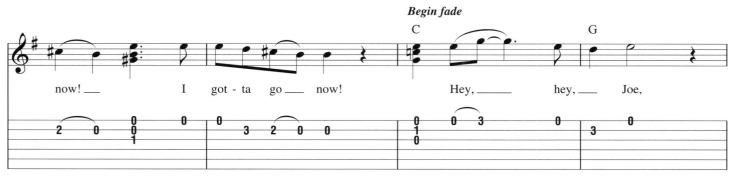

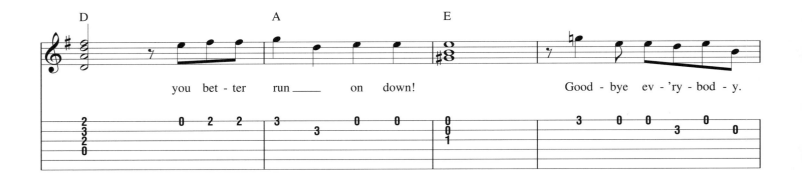

you bet - ter run _____ on down!   Good - bye ev - 'ry - bod - y.

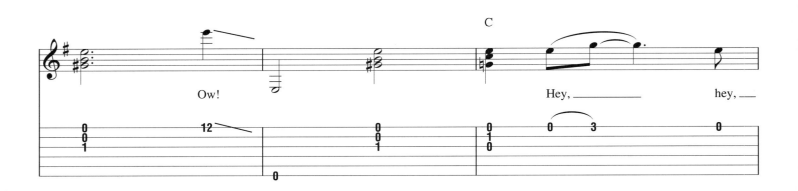

Ow!   Hey, _____ hey, _____

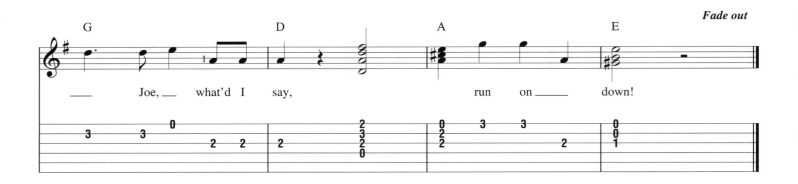

_____ Joe, _____ what'd I say,   run on _____ down!

Additional Lyrics

2. Uh, hey, Joe, I heard you shot your woman down,
   You shot her down now.
   Uh, hey, Joe, I heard you shot your old lady down,
   You shot her down in the ground. Yeah!
   Yes I did, I shot her,
   You know I caught her messin' 'round, messin' 'round town.
   Uh, yes I did, I shot her,
   You know I caught my old lady messin' 'round town.
   And I gave her the gun, I shot her!

3. Hey, Joe, said now, uh, where you gonna run to now,
   Where you gonna run to? Yeah.
   Hey, Joe, I said, where you gonna run to now, where you,
   Where you gonna go? Well, dig it!
   I'm goin' way down south, way down to Mexico way! Alright!
   I'm goin' way down south, way down where I can be free!
   Ain't no one gonna find me, babe!

Layla

Words and Music by Eric Clapton and Jim Gordon

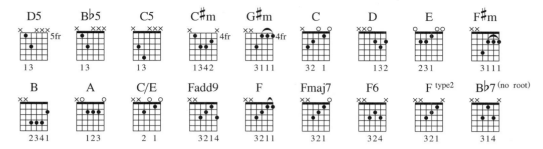

Strum Pattern: 1
Pick Pattern: 3, 5

Intro

Moderately fast

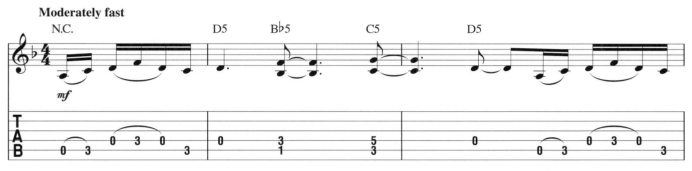

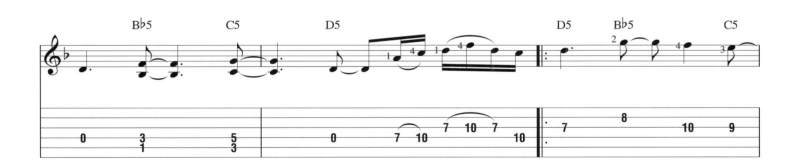

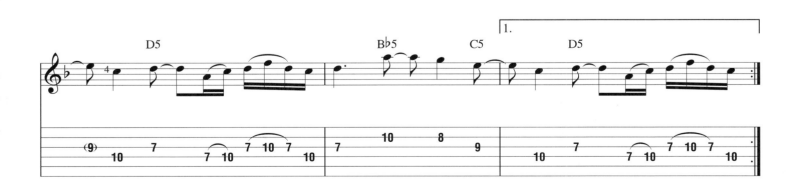

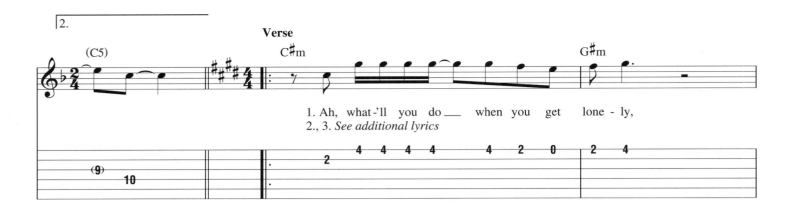

1. Ah, what -'ll you do ___ when you get lone - ly,
2., 3. *See additional lyrics*

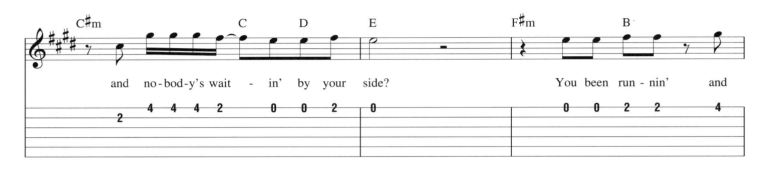

and no-bod-y's wait - in' by your side? You been run - nin' and

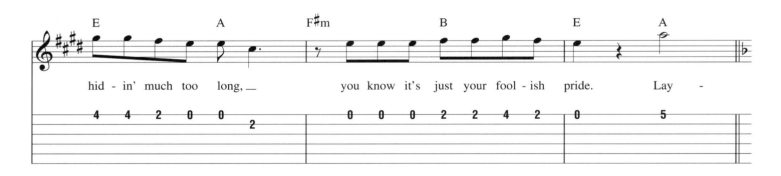

hid - in' much too long, ___ you know it's just your fool - ish pride. Lay -

Chorus

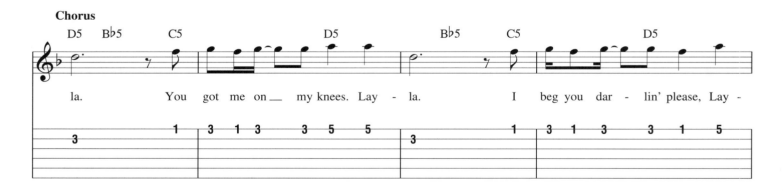

la. You got me on ___ my knees. Lay - la. I beg you dar - lin' please, Lay -

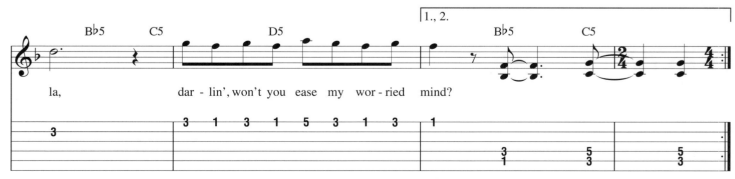

la, dar - lin', won't you ease my wor - ried mind?

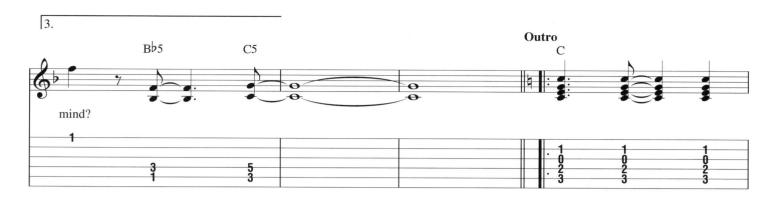

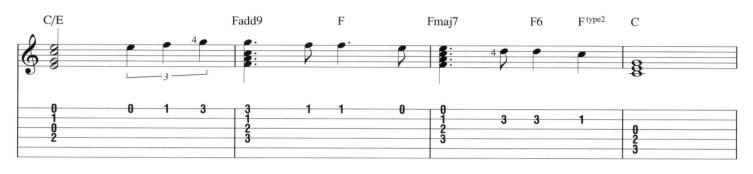

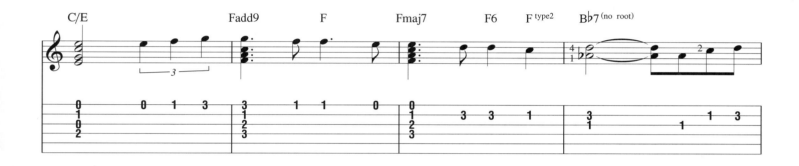

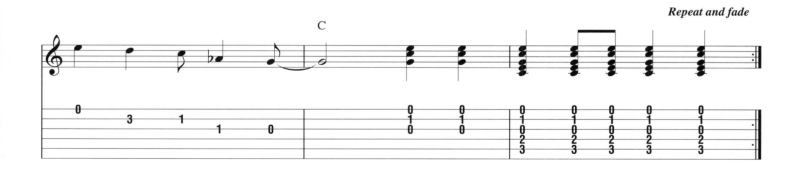

Additional Lyrics

2. I tried to give you consolation
   When your old man, he let you down.
   Like a fool, I fell in love with you,
   You turned my whole world upside down.

3. So make the best of the situation,
   Before I fin'lly go insane.
   Please don't say we'll never find a way,
   And tell me all my love's in vain.

Message in a Bottle

Music and Lyrics by Sting

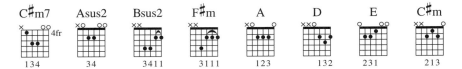

Strum Pattern: 6
Pick Pattern: 4

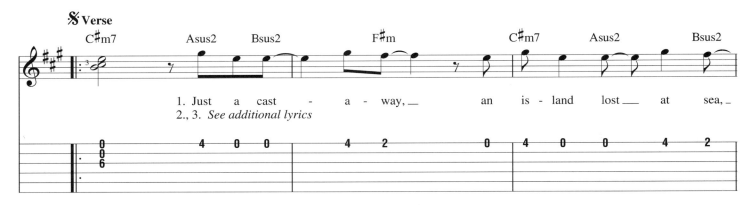

1. Just a cast - a - way, __ an is - land lost __ at sea, __
2., 3. *See additional lyrics*

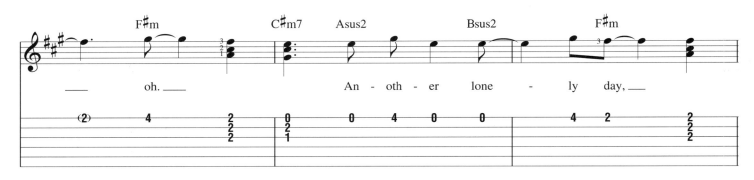

__ oh. __ An - oth - er lone - ly day, __

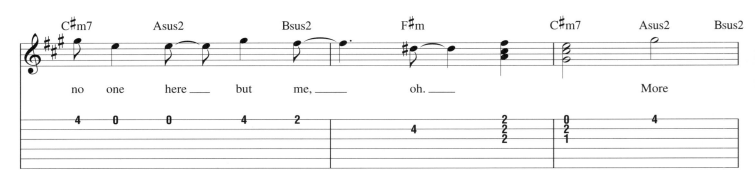

no one here __ but me, __ oh. __ More

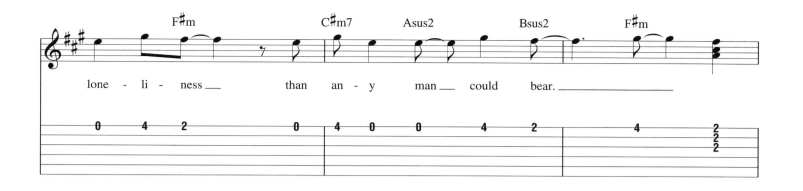

lone - li - ness ___ than an - y man ___ could bear. _____

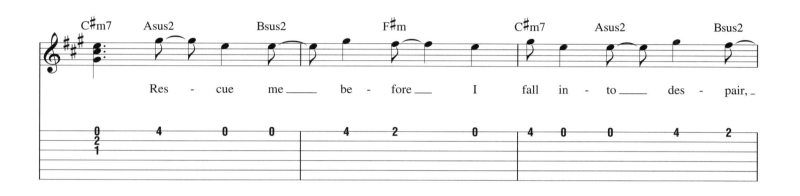

Res - cue me ___ be - fore ___ I fall in - to ___ des - pair, _

Pre-Chorus

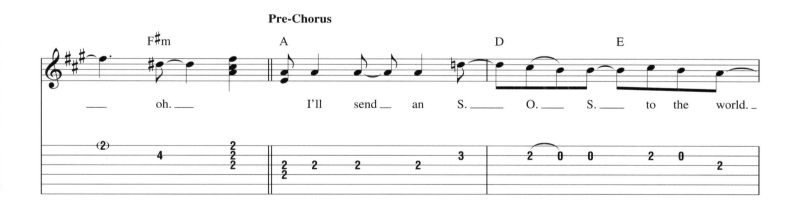

___ oh. ___ I'll send ___ an S. ___ O. ___ S. ___ to the world. _

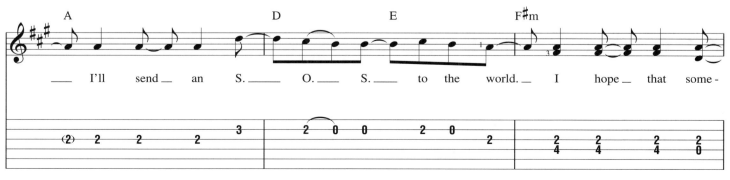

___ I'll send ___ an S. ___ O. ___ S. ___ to the world. _ I hope ___ that some -

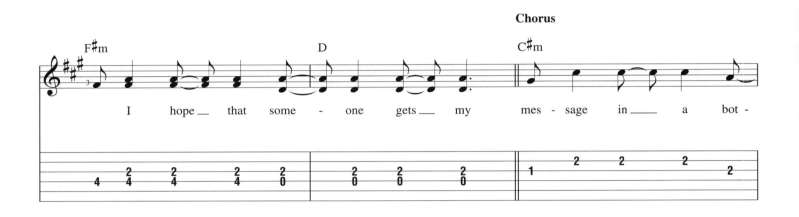

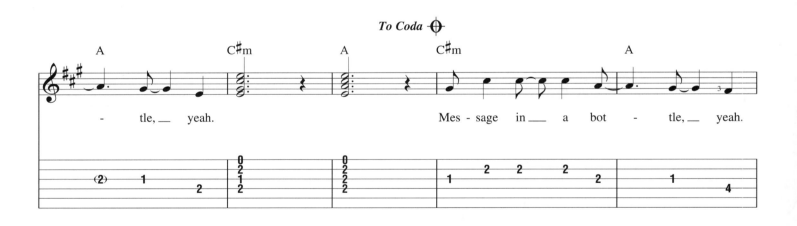

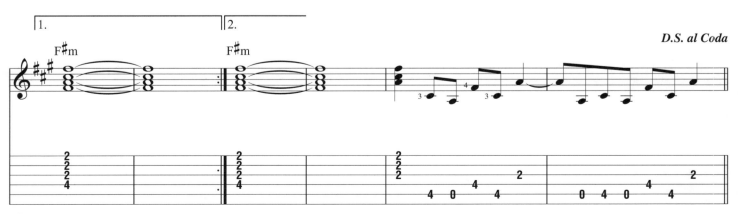

Coda

Outro

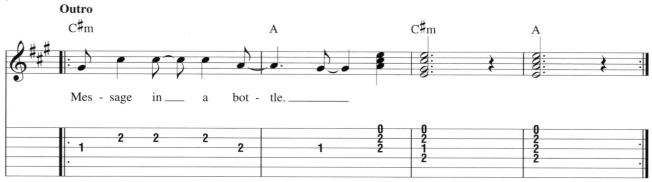

Mes - sage in ____ a bot - tle. _____

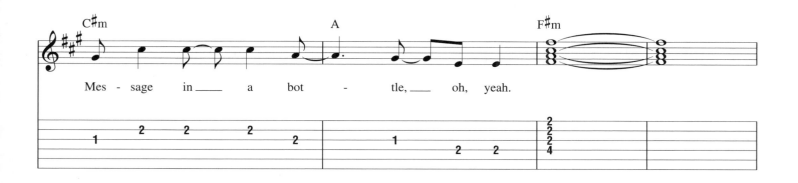

Mes - sage in ____ a bot - tle, ___ oh, yeah.

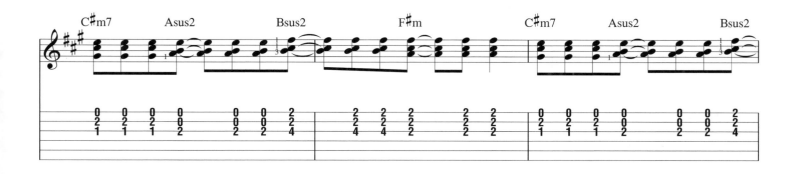

Repeat and fade

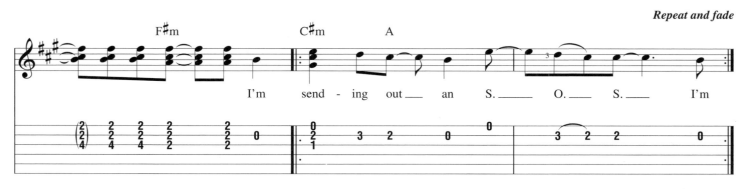

I'm send - ing out ___ an S. _____ O. ___ S. ___ I'm

Additional Lyrics

2. A year has passed since I wrote my note,
   But I should have known this right from the start.
   Only hope can keep me together.
   Love can mend your life but love can break your heart.

3. Walked out this morning, I don't believe what I saw,
   A hundred billion bottles washed up on the shore.
   Seems like I'm not alone at being alone.
   A hundred billion castaways looking for a home.

Rebel, Rebel

Words and Music by David Bowie

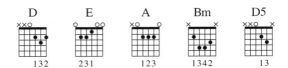

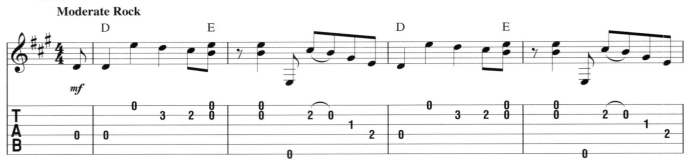

Strum Pattern: 4
Pick Pattern: 1

Intro
Moderate Rock

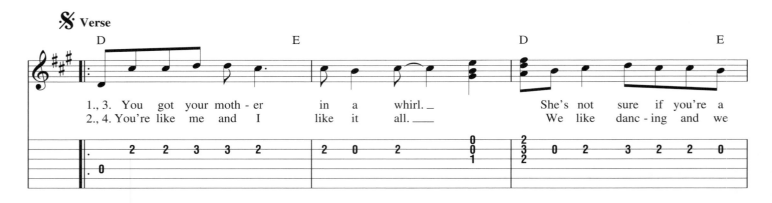

Doo, doo, doo, doot, doo, doo, doo, doo.

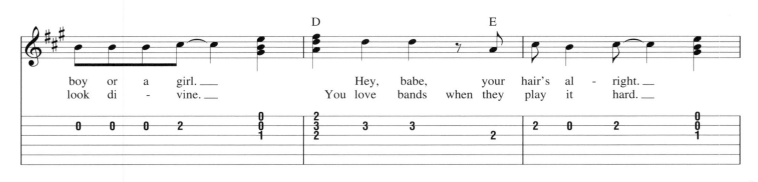

Verse

1., 3. You got your moth - er in a whirl. __ She's not sure if you're a
2., 4. You're like me and I like it all. __ We like danc - ing and we

boy or a girl. __ Hey, babe, your hair's al - right. __
look di - vine. __ You love bands when they play it hard. __

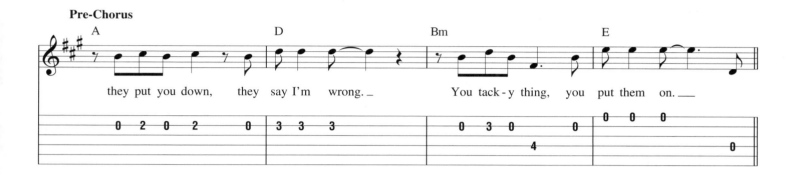

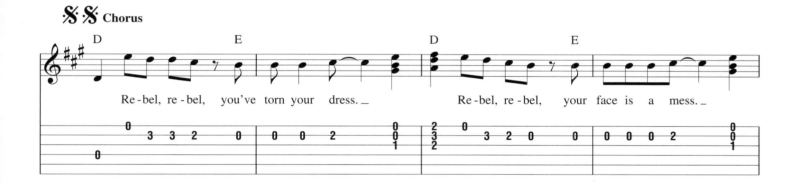

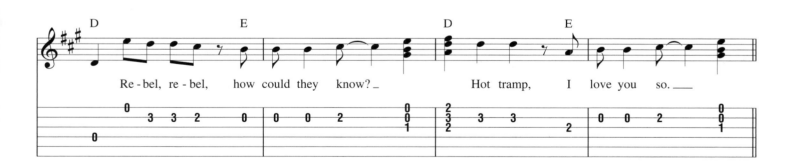

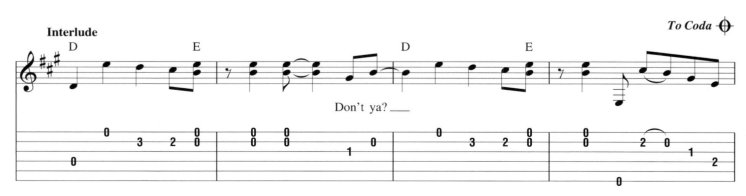

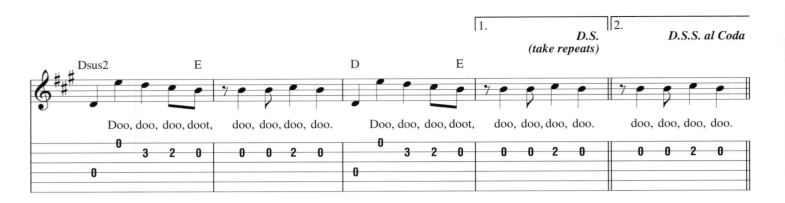

⊕ Coda

Outro-Chorus

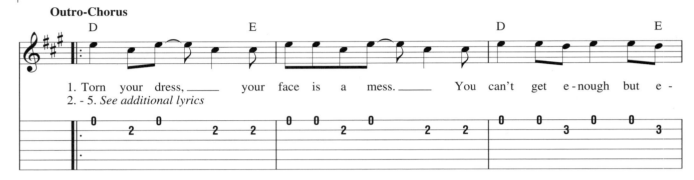

1. Torn your dress, ____ your face is a mess. ____ You can't get e-nough but e-
2. - 5. *See additional lyrics*

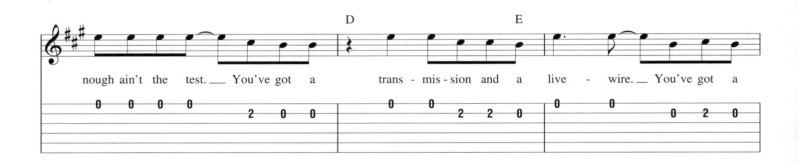

nough ain't the test. __ You've got a trans-mis-sion and a live - wire. __ You've got a

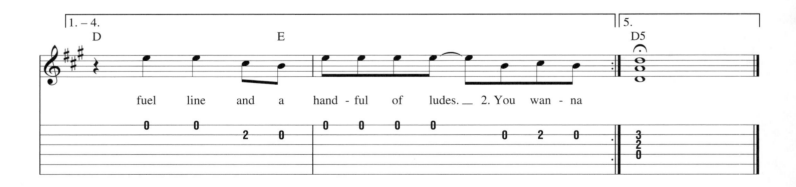

fuel line and a hand-ful of ludes. __ 2. You wan - na

Additional Lyrics

2. You wanna be there when they count up the dudes
   And I love your dress.
   You're a juvenile success
   Because your face is a mess.

3. So, how could they know?
   I said, "How could they know?
   So what you want to know?
   Where you want to go?

4. What can I do for you?
   Looks like I've been there too.
   Because you've torn your dress.
   And your face is a mess.
   Ooh, your face is a mess, oh, oh.

5. So how could they know?
   How could they know?

Rhiannon

Words and Music by Stevie Nicks

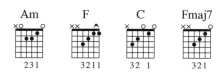

Strum Pattern: 6
Pick Pattern: 2

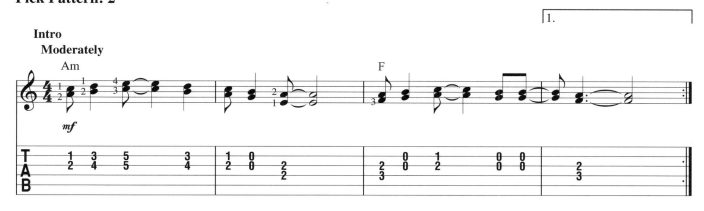

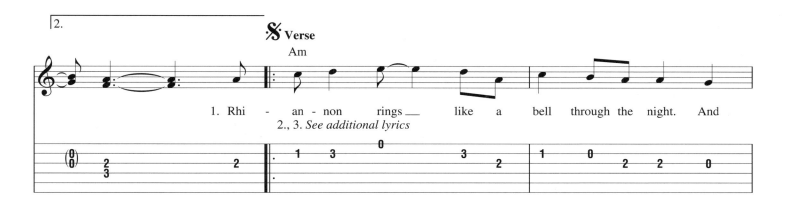

1. Rhi - an - non rings ___ like a bell through the night. And
2., 3. See additional lyrics

would - n't you love ___ to love ___ her? Takes to the sky like a

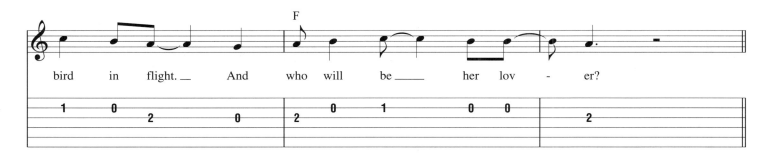

bird in flight. ___ And who will be ___ her lov - er?

Pre-Chorus

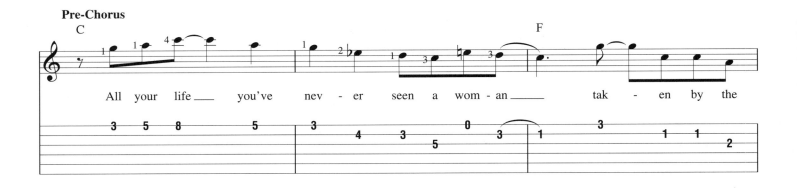

All your life ___ you've nev - er seen a wom - an ___ tak - en by the

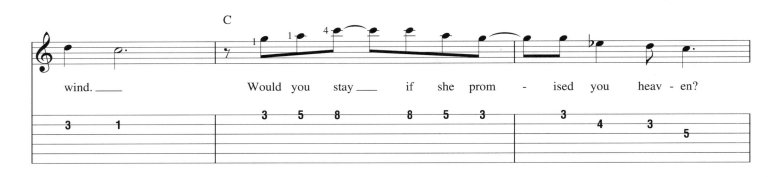

wind. ___ Would you stay ___ if she prom - ised you heav - en?

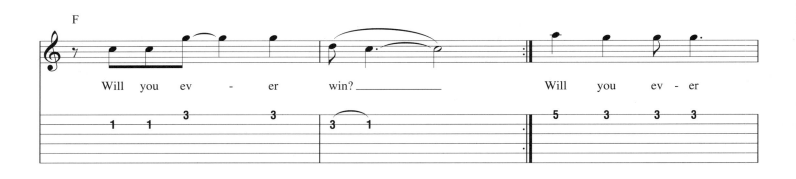

Will you ev - er win? ___ Will you ev - er

To Coda ✛

Chorus

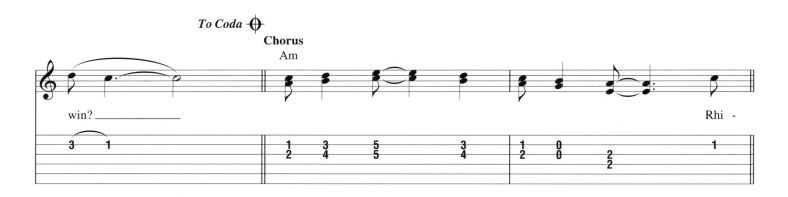

win? ___ Rhi -

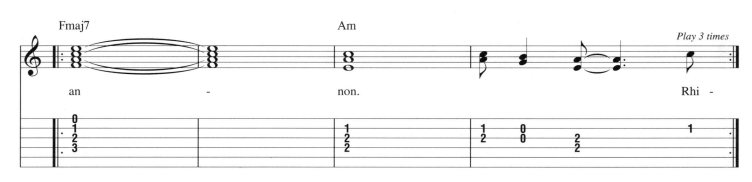

an - non. Rhi -

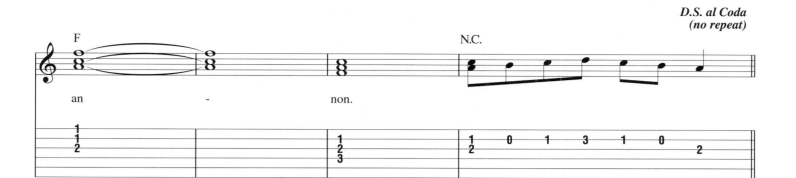

an - non.

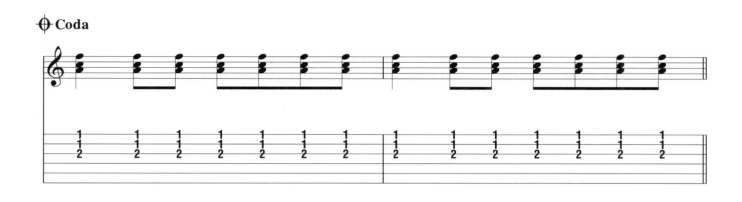

⊕ Coda

Outro

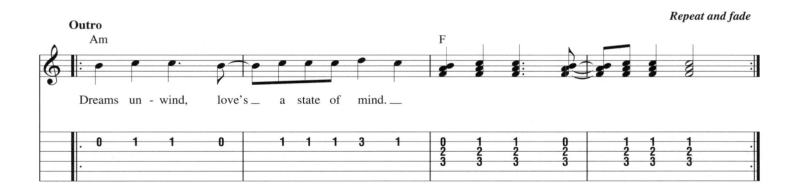

Dreams un - wind, love's _ a state of mind. _

Additional Lyrics

2. She is like a cat in the dark.
   And then she is the darkness.
   She rules her life like a flying skylark.
   And when the sky is starlets.

3. She rings like a bell through the night.
   And wouldn't you love to love her?
   She rules her life like a bird in flight.
   And who will be her lover?

Refugee

Words and Music by Tom Petty and Mike Campbell

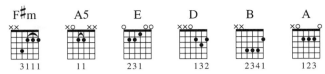

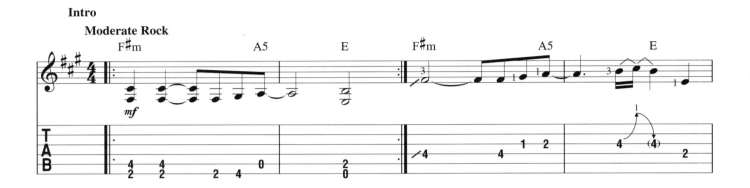

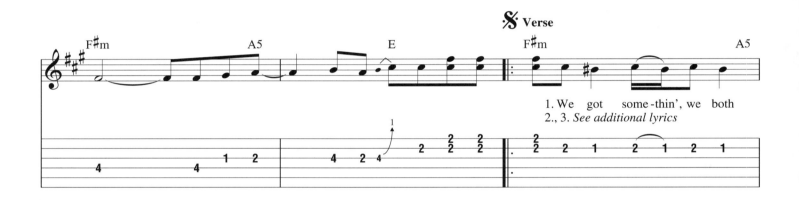

1. We got some-thin', we both know it, we don't talk too much a-bout ___ it.
2., 3. *See additional lyrics*

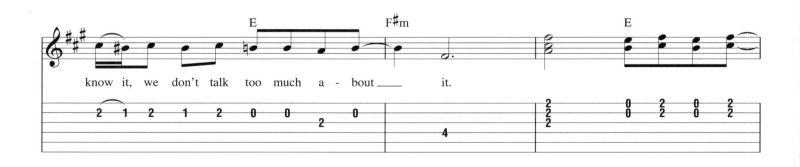

know it, we don't talk too much a-bout ___ it.

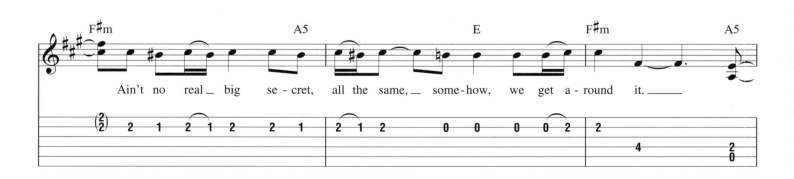

Ain't no real ___ big se-cret, all the same, ___ some-how, we get a-round it. ___

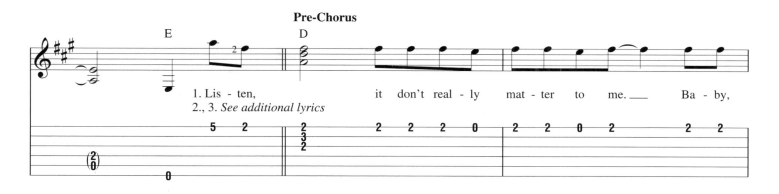

Pre-Chorus

1. Lis - ten, it don't real - ly mat - ter to me. __ Ba - by,
2., 3. *See additional lyrics*

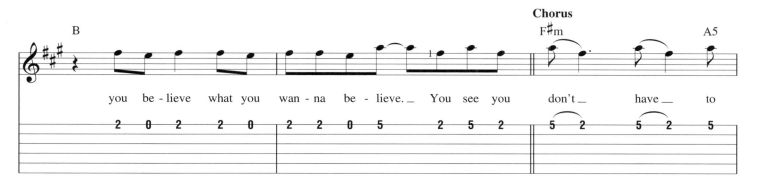

Chorus

you be - lieve what you wan - na be - lieve. __ You see you don't __ have __ to

To Coda ⊕ | 1.

live like a ref - u - gee. (Don't have to live like a ref - u - gee.) __

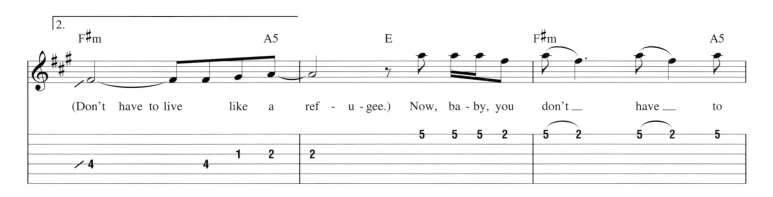

2.

(Don't have to live like a ref - u - gee.) Now, ba - by, you don't __ have __ to

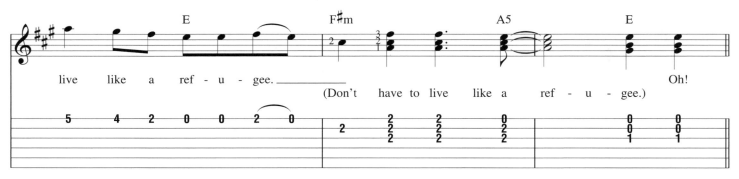

live like a ref - u - gee. __ Oh!

(Don't have to live like a ref - u - gee.)

Bridge

Ba - by, we ain't the first. __ I'm sure a lot of oth - er

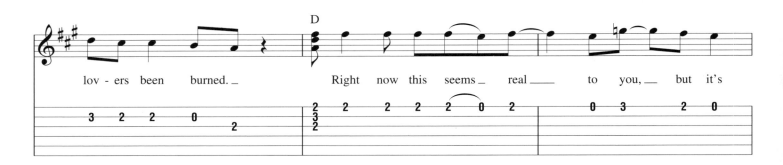

lov - ers been burned. __ Right now this seems __ real __ to you, __ but it's

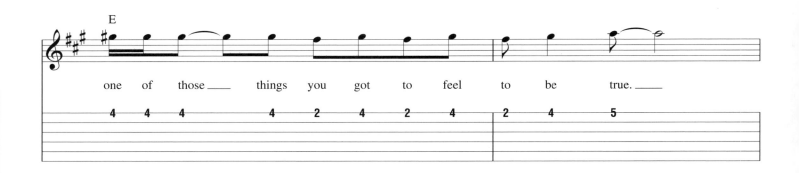

one of those __ things you got to feel to be true. __

4th time, D.S. al Coda

Guitar Solo

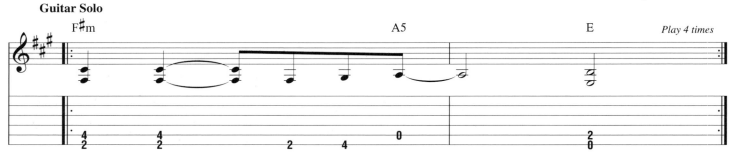

Coda

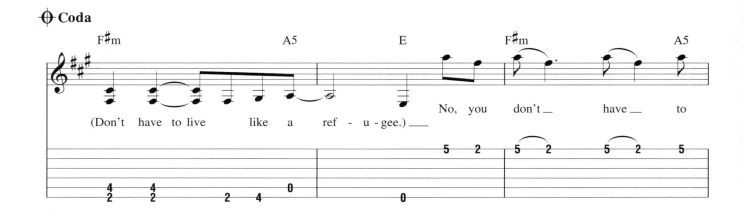

(Don't have to live like a ref - u - gee.) __ No, you don't __ have __ to

42

live   like   a   ref - u - gee.   (Don't   have   to   live   like   a   ref - u - gee.) ___   Ba - by, you

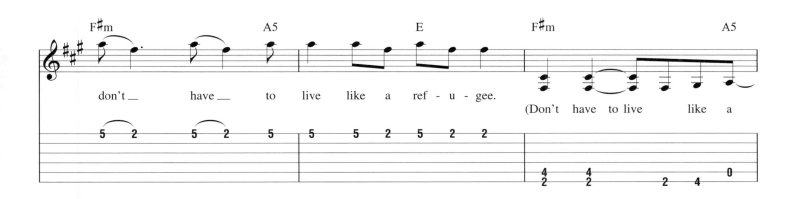

don't ___   have ___   to   live   like   a   ref - u - gee.   (Don't   have   to   live   like   a

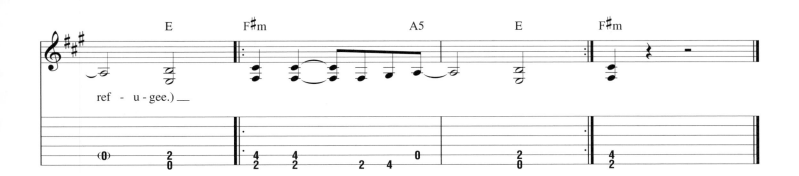

ref - u - gee.) ___

Additional Lyrics

2. Somewhere, somehow,
    Somebody must have kicked you around some.
    Tell me why you wanna lay there,
    Revel in your abandon.

Pre-Chorus 2. Honey, it don't make no diff'rence to me.
                 Baby, ev'rybody's had to fight to be free.

3. Somewhere, somehow,
    Somebody must have kicked you around some.
    Who knows? Maybe you were kidnapped,
    Tied up, taken away and held for ransom.

Pre-Chorus 3. Honey, it don't really matter to me.
                 Baby, ev'rybody's had to fight to be free.

Rock and Roll Never Forgets

Words and Music by Bob Seger

Strum Pattern: 2, 3

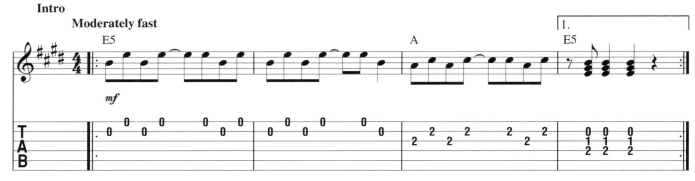

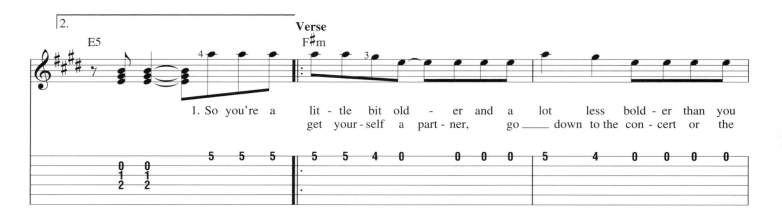

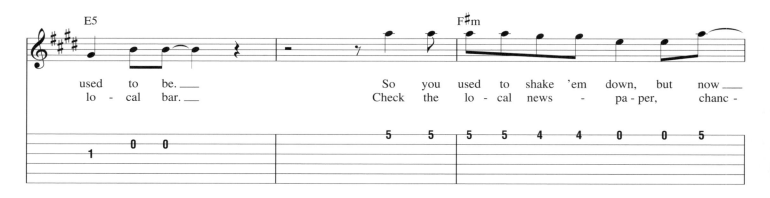

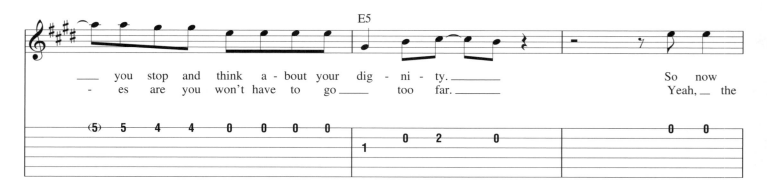

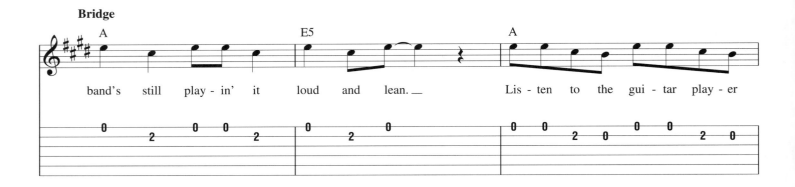

Bridge

band's still play - in' it loud and lean. __ Lis - ten to the gui - tar play - er

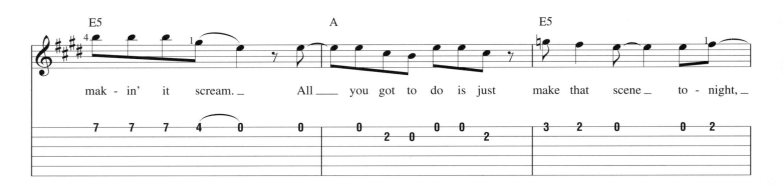

mak - in' it scream. __ All __ you got to do is just make that scene __ to - night, __

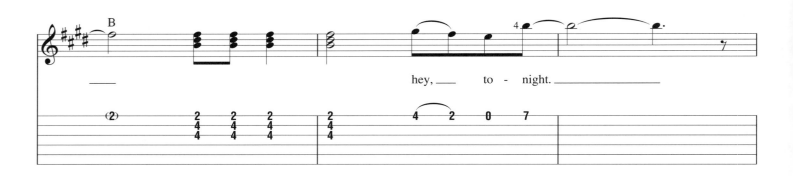

hey, __ to - night. _____

Guitar Solo

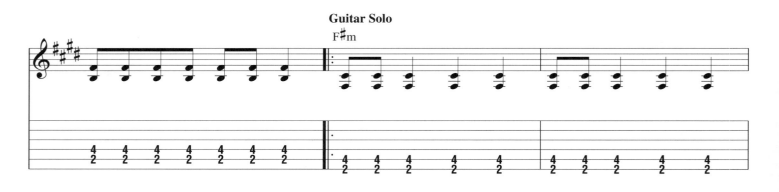

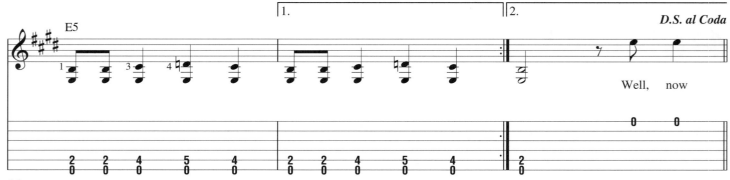

D.S. al Coda

Well, now

⊕ Coda

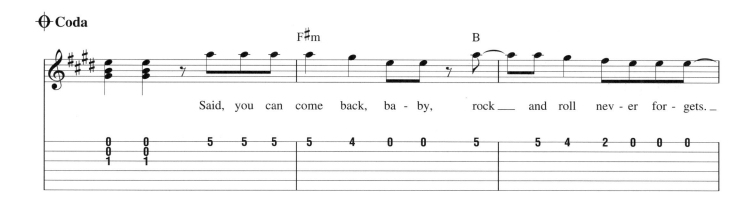

Said, you can come back, ba - by, rock __ and roll nev - er for - gets. __

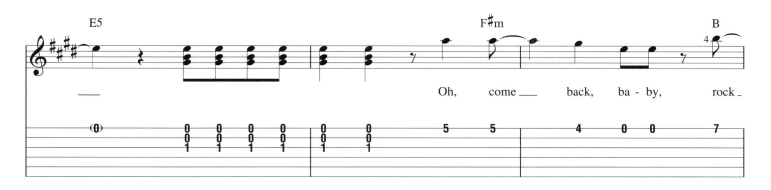

Oh, come __ back, ba - by, rock __

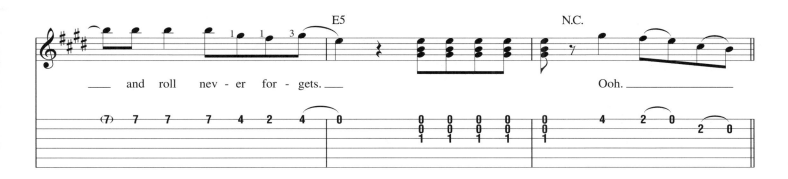

__ and roll nev - er for - gets. __ Ooh. __

Interlude
w/ Lead Voc. ad lib.

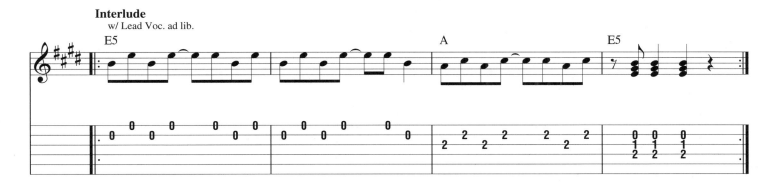

Outro
w/ Lead Voc. ad lib.

Repeat and fade

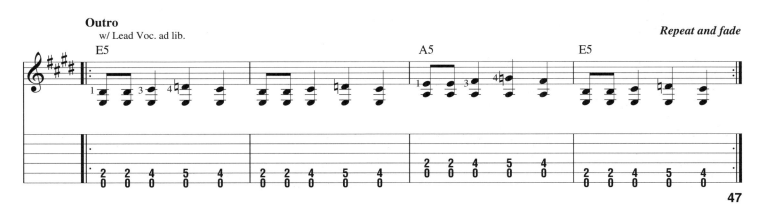

47

Run to You

Words and Music by Bryan Adams and Jim Vallance

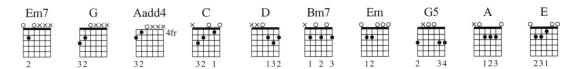

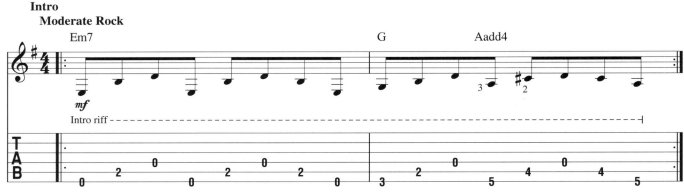

*Capo II

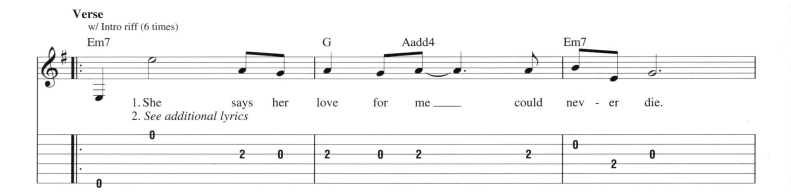

*Optional: To match recording, place capo at 2nd fret.

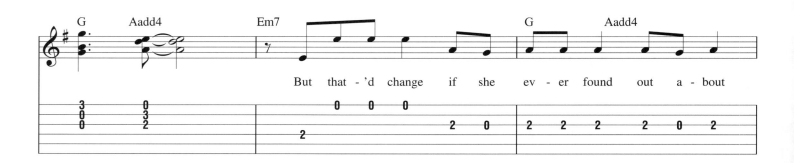

1. She says her love for me ____ could nev - er die.
2. *See additional lyrics*

But that - 'd change if she ev - er found out a - bout

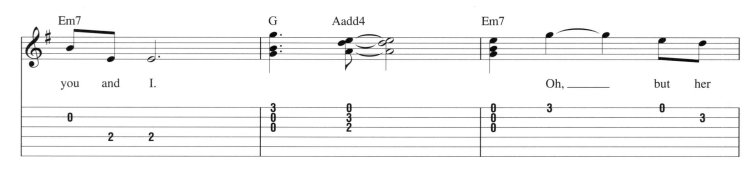

you and I. Oh, _____ but her

love is cold. _____ Would-n't hurt her if she did-n't know, _ 'cause...

Strum Pattern: 6
Pick Pattern: 4

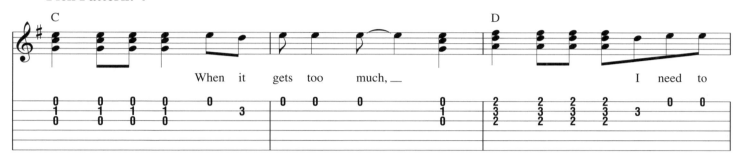

When it gets too much, _ I need to

𝄋 **Chorus**

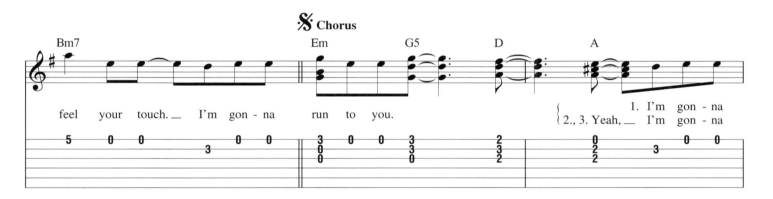

feel your touch. _ I'm gon-na run to you.

1. I'm gon-na
2., 3. Yeah, _ I'm gon-na

run to you.   'Cause when the feel-in's right _ I'm gon-na
run to you.   'Cause when the feel-in's right _ I'm gon-na

To Coda ⊕ | 1.

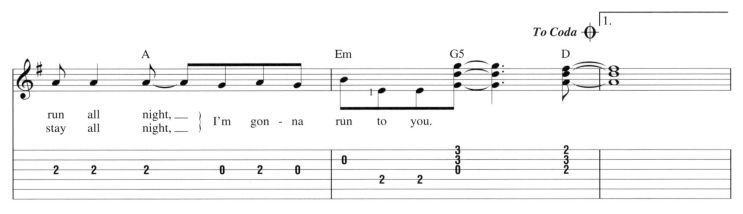

run all night, _ } I'm gon-na run to you.
stay all night, _

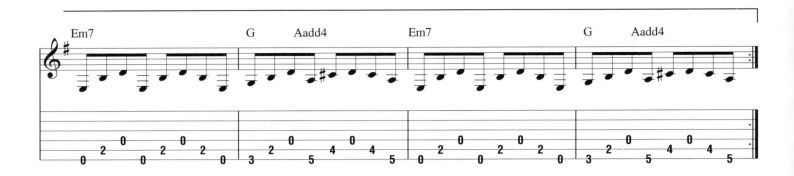

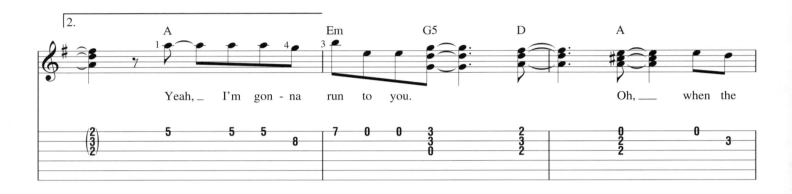

Yeah, __ I'm gon - na run to you. Oh, __ when the

feel - in's right, __ I'm gon - na run all night, __ I'm gon - na run to you. __

Interlude

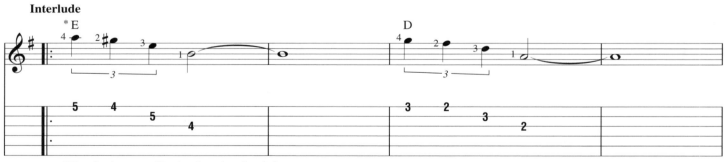

*Play chords once and let ring throughout Interlude.

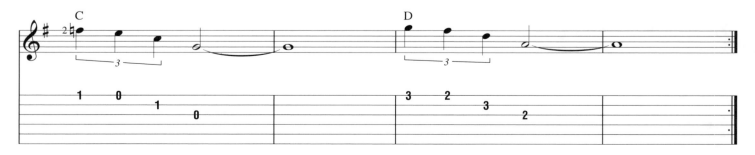

Pre-Chorus

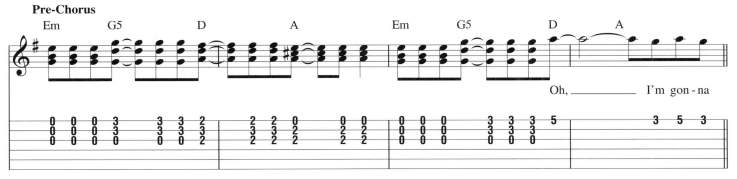

⊕ Coda

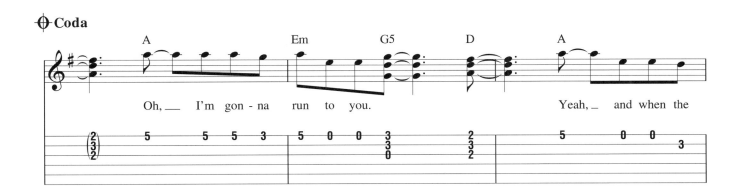

Repeat and fade

Outro

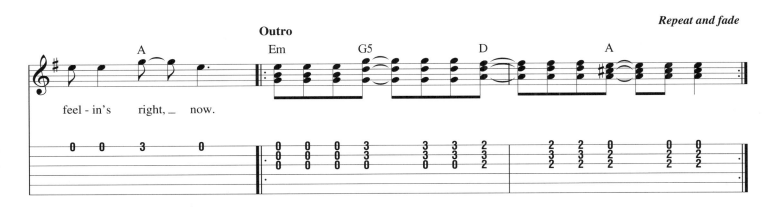

Additional Lyrics

2. She's got a heart of gold, she'd never let me down.
But you're the one that always turns me on, you keep me comin' 'round.
I know her love is true, but it's so damn easy makin' love to you.
I got my mind made up, I need to feel your touch.

Smoke on the Water

Words and Music by Ritchie Blackmore, Ian Gillan, Roger Glover, Jon Lord and Ian Paice

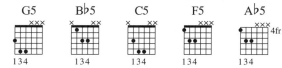

Strum Pattern: 1, 3
Pick Pattern: 3, 4

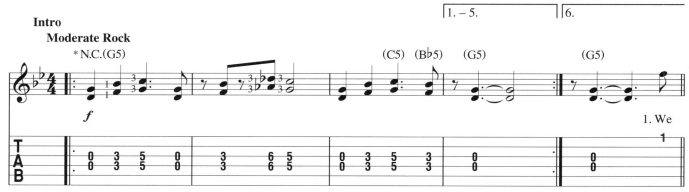

*Chords implied by bass, 3rd time.

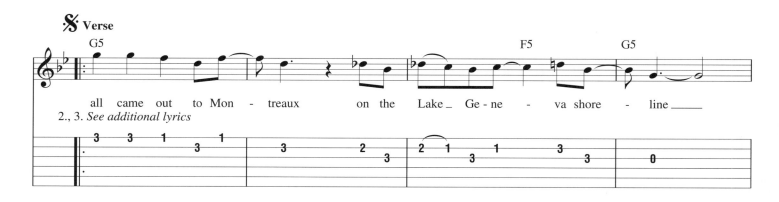

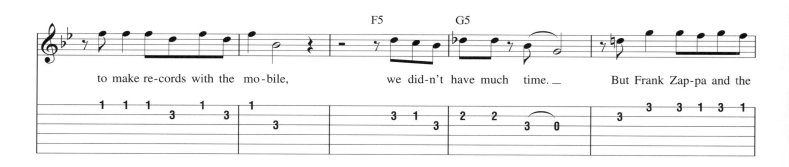

Chorus

burned the place to the ground. ___ Smoke on the wa - ter,

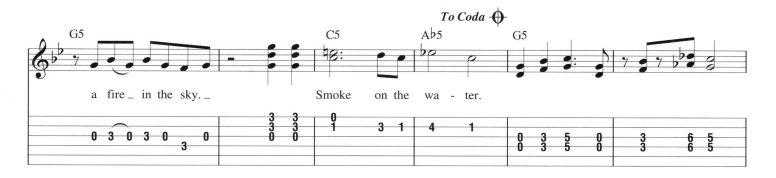

To Coda ⊕

a fire ___ in the sky. ___ Smoke on the wa - ter.

2nd time, D.S. al Coda

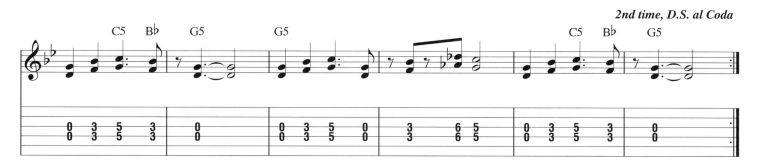

⊕ **Coda**

Repeat and fade

Outro

Additional Lyrics

2. They burned down the gambling house,
   It died with an awful sound.
   A Funky Claude was running in and out,
   Pulling kids out the ground.
   When it all was over,
   We had to find another place.
   But Swiss time was running out;
   It seemed that we would lose the race.

3. We ended up at the Grand Hotel,
   It was empty, cold and bare.
   But with the Rolling truck Stones thing just outside,
   Making our music there.
   With a few red lights, a few old beds
   We made a place to sweat.
   No matter what we get out of this,
   I know, I know we'll never forget.

Start Me Up

Words and Music by Mick Jagger and Keith Richards

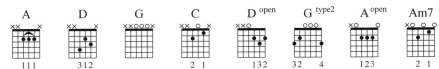

Strum Pattern: 3
Pick Pattern: 3

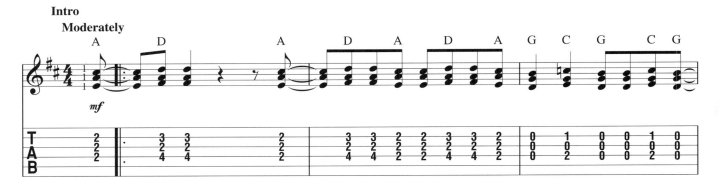

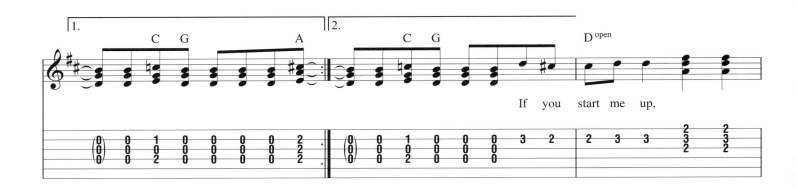

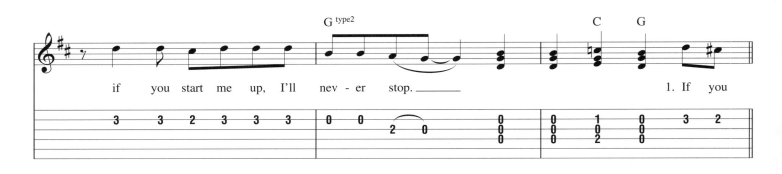

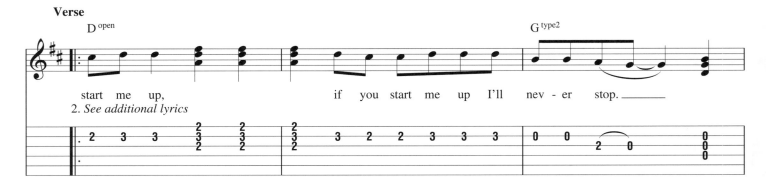

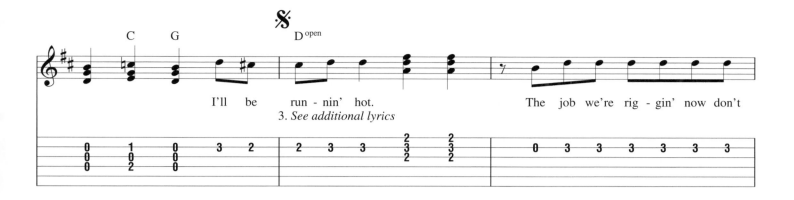

I'll be run-nin' hot.
3. See additional lyrics

The job we're rig-gin' now don't

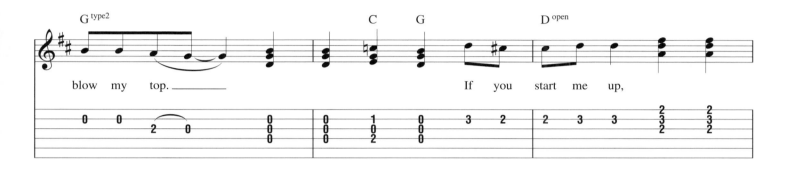

blow my top. _____ If you start me up,

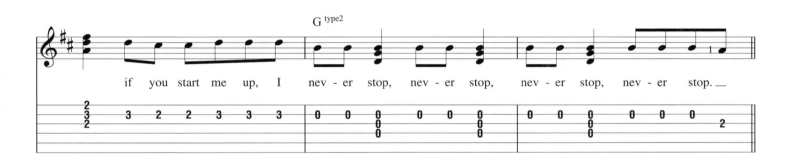

if you start me up, I nev-er stop, nev-er stop, nev-er stop, nev-er stop. __

Chorus

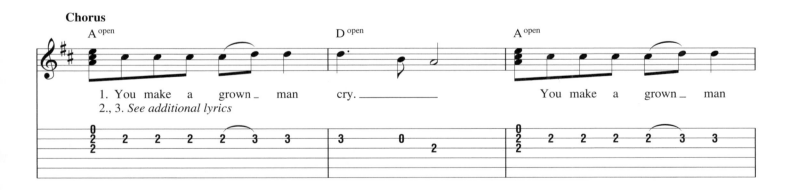

1. You make a grown _ man cry. _____
2., 3. See additional lyrics

You make a grown _ man

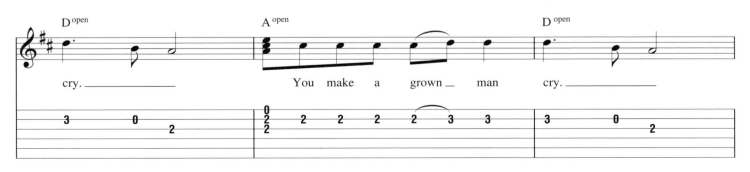

cry. _____ You make a grown _ man cry. _____

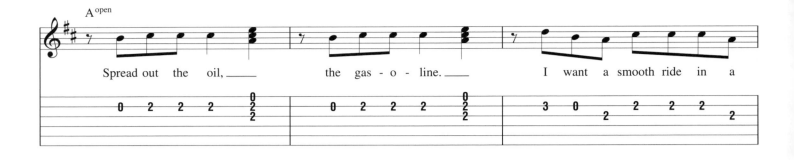

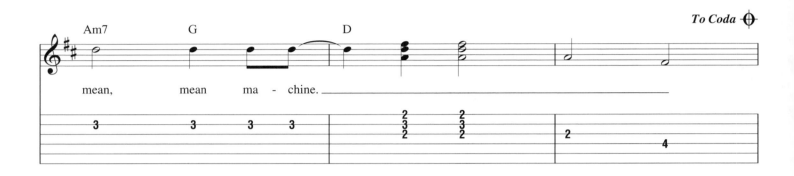

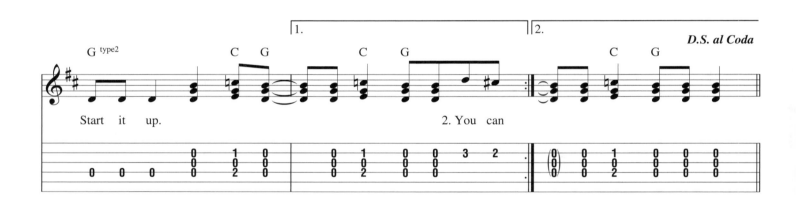

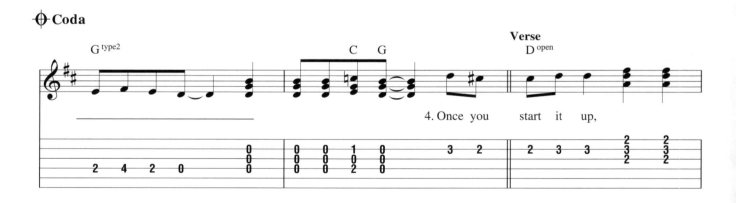

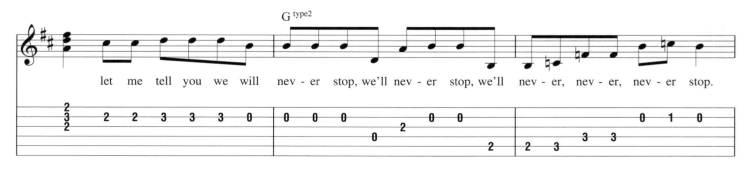

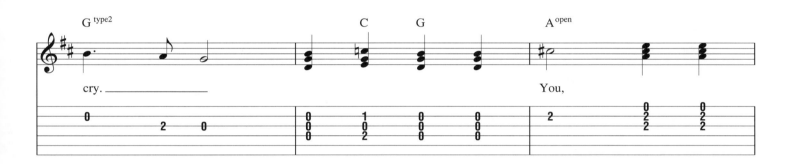

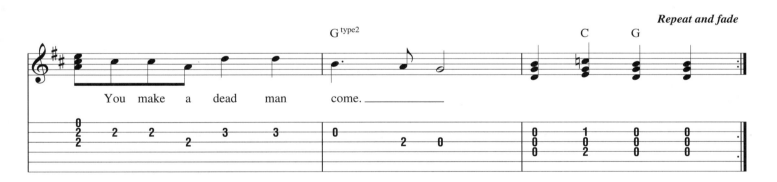

Additional Lyrics

2. You can start me up. Kick on the starter, give it all you've got, you've got, you've got.
I can't compete with the riders in the other heats.
You rough it up, if you like it, you can start it up, start it up, start it up, start it up.

Chorus 2. Don't make a grown man cry. Don't make a grown man cry.
Don't make a grown man cry. My eyes dilate, my lips go green,
My hands are greasy, she's a mean, mean machine. Start it up.

3. Start me up. Now, give it all you've got, you've got to, never, never, never stop.
Start it up. Whoo! Oh, baby, why don't ya start it up? Never, never, never.

Chorus 3. You make a grown man cry. You make a grown man cry.
You make a grown man cry. Ride like the wind at double speed,
I'll take you places that you've never, never seen.

Surrender

Words and Music by Rick Nielsen

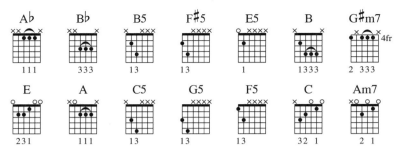

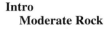

Strum Pattern: 1
Pick Pattern: 4

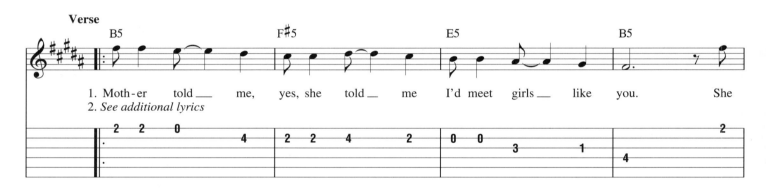

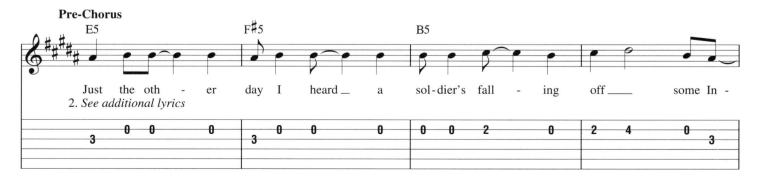

-do - ne - sian junk that's go - ing 'round. _____

Chorus

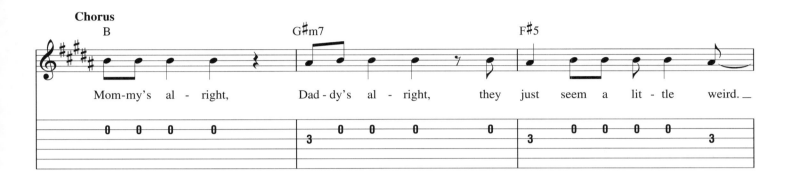

Mom-my's al - right, Dad - dy's al - right, they just seem a lit - tle weird. _

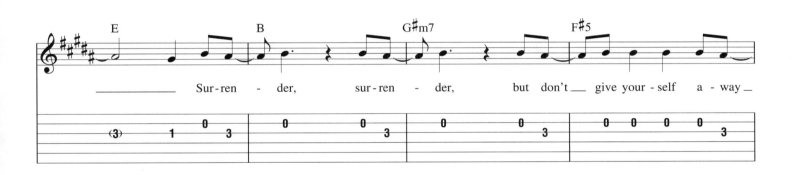

_____ Sur-ren - der, sur-ren - der, but don't __ give your-self a - way __

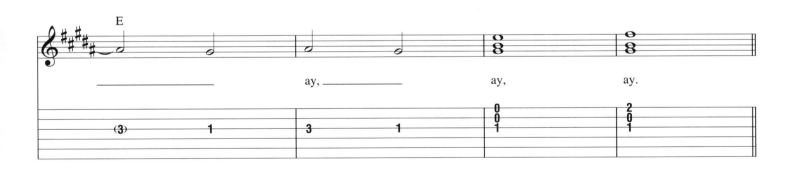

_____ ay, _____ ay, ay.

Interlude

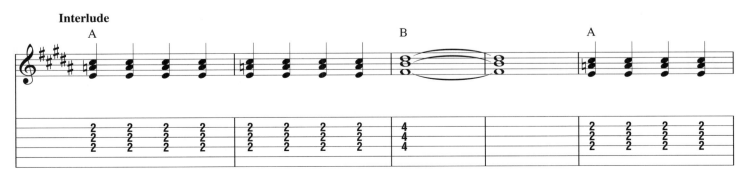

59

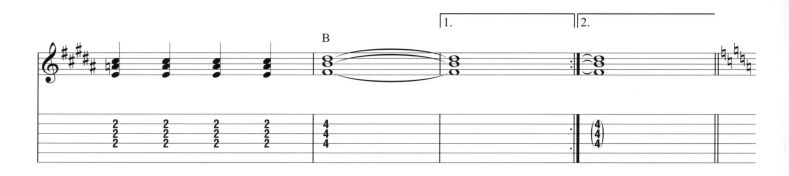

Verse

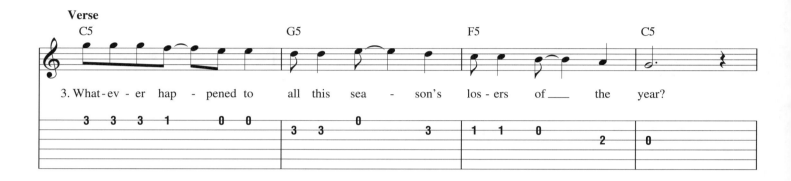

3. What-ev-er hap - pened to all this sea - son's los - ers of ___ the year?

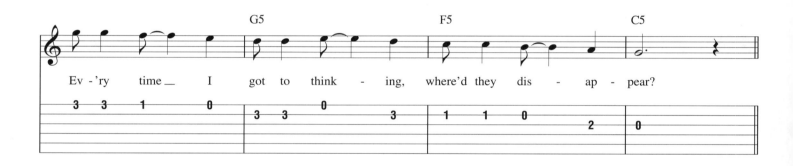

Ev-'ry time ___ I got to think - ing, where'd they dis - ap - pear?

Pre-Chorus

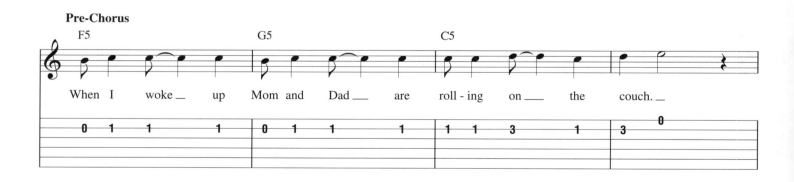

When I woke ___ up Mom and Dad ___ are roll - ing on ___ the couch. ___

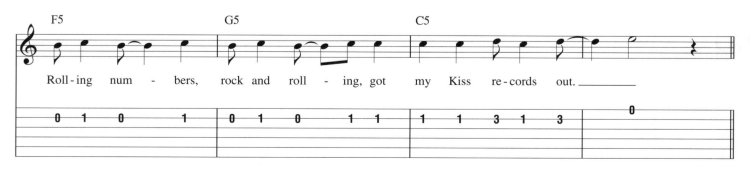

Roll - ing num - bers, rock and roll - ing, got my Kiss re-cords out. ___

Chorus

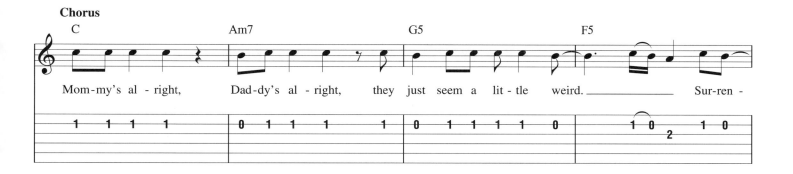

Mom-my's al-right, Dad-dy's al-right, they just seem a lit-tle weird. _____ Sur-ren-

-der, sur-ren-der, but don't __ give your-self a-way _____ ay, _____

Bridge

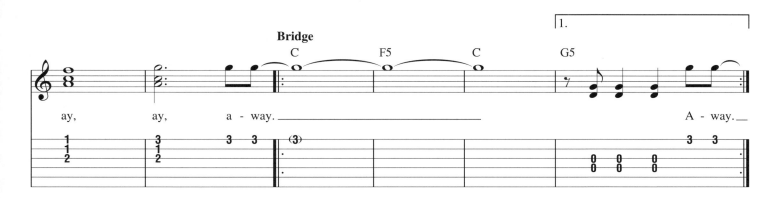

ay, ay, a-way. _____ A-way._

2.

Outro-Chorus *Repeat and fade*

Sur-ren - der sur-ren - der, but don't __ give your-self a-way. _____ Sur-ren-

Additional Lyrics

2. Father says, "Your mother's right,
   She's really up on things.
   Before we married, mommy served
   In the WACS in the Philippines."

Pre-Chorus Now I had heard the WACS recruited
   Old maids for the war.
   But mommy isn't one of those,
   I've known her all these years.

Tush

Words and Music by Billy F Gibbons, Dusty Hill and Frank Beard

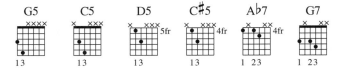

Strum Pattern: 1

Intro

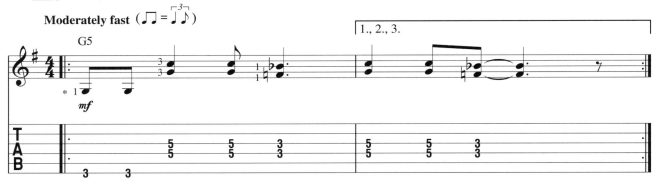

*Optional; Thumb on 6th string

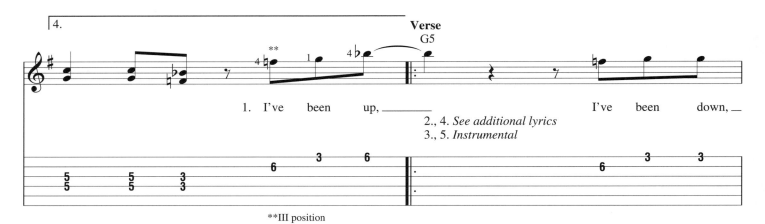

1. I've been up, _____ I've been down, _____

2., 4. *See additional lyrics*
3., 5. *Instrumental*

**III position

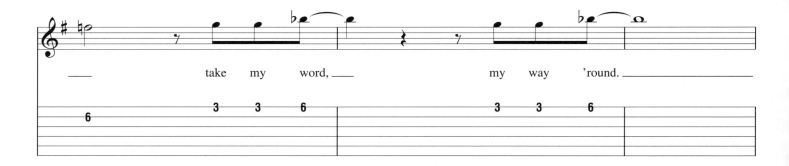

_____ take my word, _____ my way 'round. _____

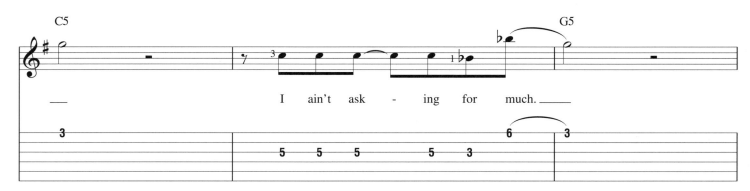

_____ I ain't ask - ing for much. _____

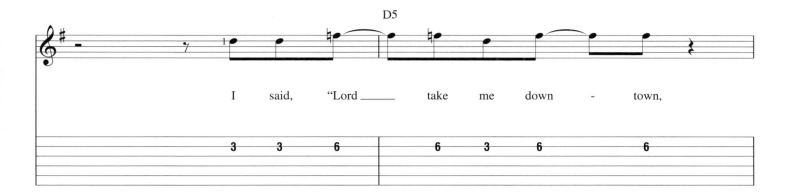

I said, "Lord _____ take me down - town,

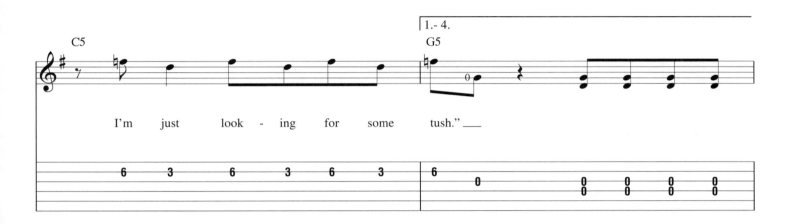

I'm just look - ing for some tush." ___

2. I've been bad, __

Additional Lyrics

2. I've been bad,
   I've been good,
   Dallas, Texas, Hollywood.
   I ain't asking for much.
   I said, "Lord take me downtown,
   I'm just looking for some tush."

4. Take me back,
   Way back home,
   Not by myself, not alone.
   I ain't asking for much.
   I said, "Lord take me downtown,
   I'm just looking for some tush."

Walk This Way

Words and Music by Steven Tyler and Joe Perry

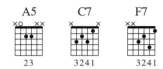

Strum Pattern: 2
Pick Pattern: 3

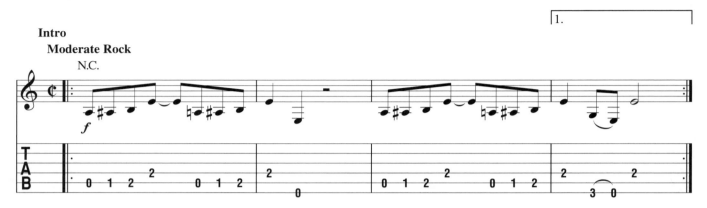

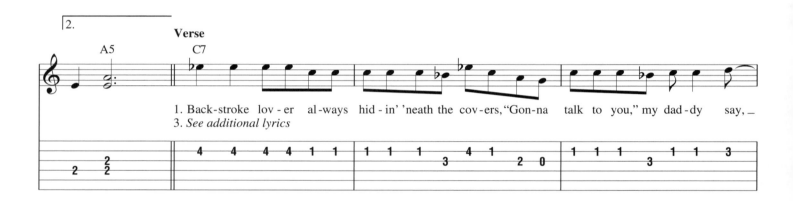

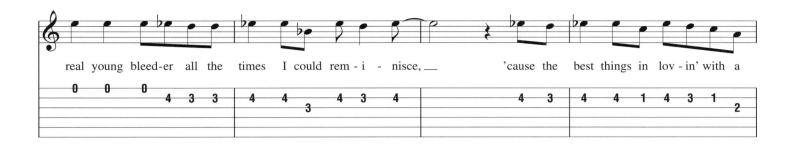

real young bleed-er all the times I could rem - i - nisce, ___ 'cause the best things in lov - in' with a

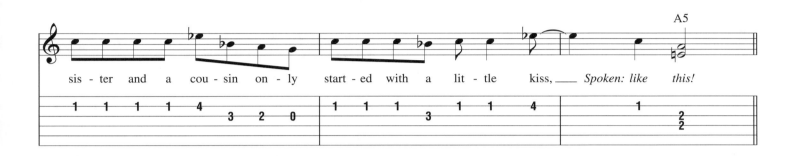

sis - ter and a cou - sin on - ly start - ed with a lit - tle kiss, ___ *Spoken: like this!*

Interlude

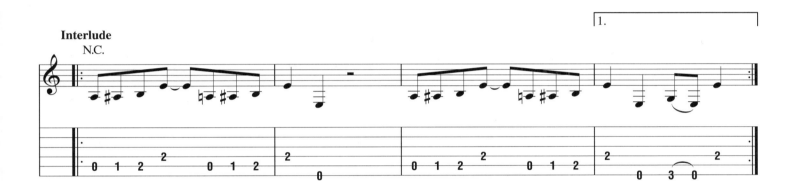

Verse

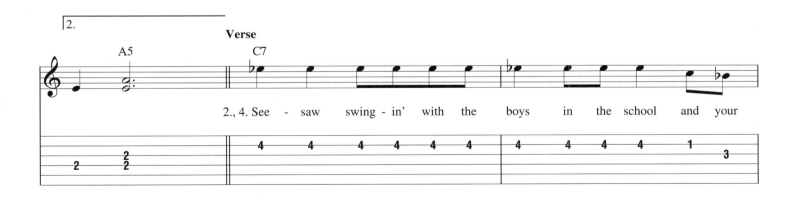

2., 4. See - saw swing - in' with the boys in the school and your

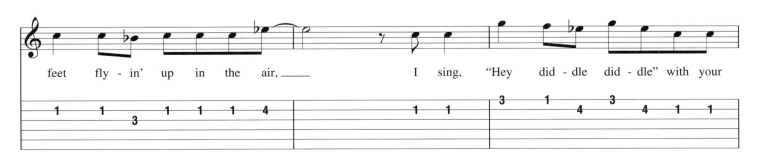

feet fly - in' up in the air, ___ I sing, "Hey did - dle did - dle" with your

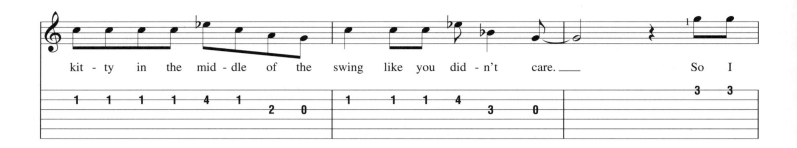

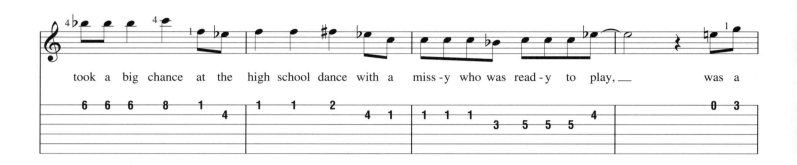

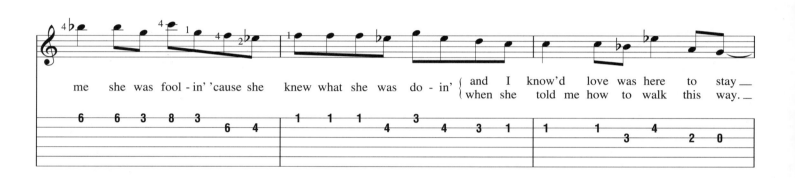

Chorus

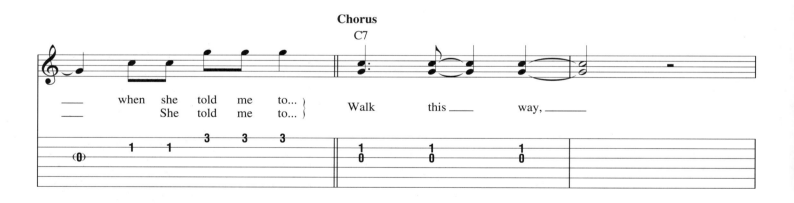

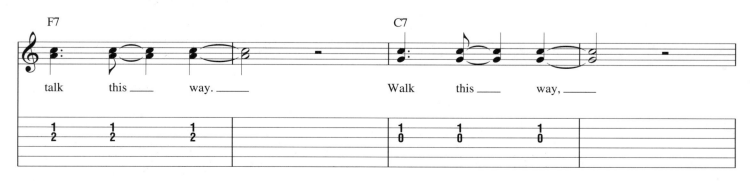

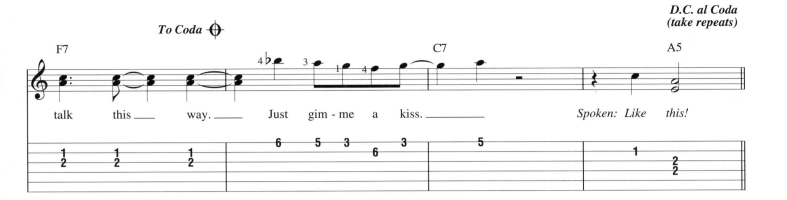

talk this ___ way. ___ Just gim - me a kiss. _____ *Spoken: Like this!*

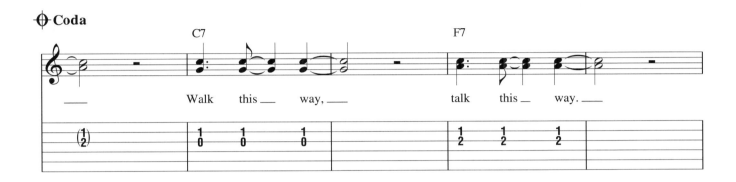

___ Walk this ___ way, ___ talk this ___ way. ___

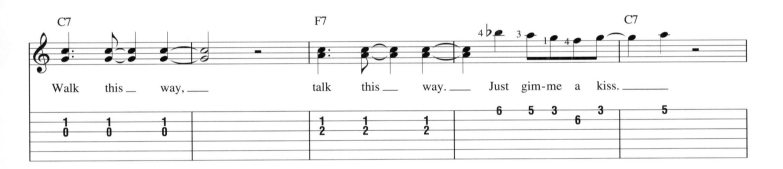

Walk this ___ way, ___ talk this ___ way. ___ Just gim - me a kiss. _____

Repeat and fade

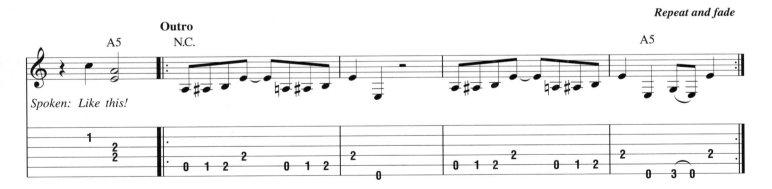

Spoken: Like this!

Additional Lyrics

3. School girl skinny with a classy kinda sassy
Little skirt's climbin' way up her knee,
There was three young ladies in the school gym locker
When I noticed they was lookin' at me.
I was a high school loser, never made it with a lady
'Til the boys told me somethin' I missed,
Then my next door neighbor with a daughter had a favor
So I gave her just a little kiss, like this!

Rock'n Me

Words and Music by Steve Miller

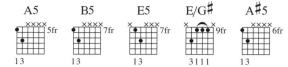

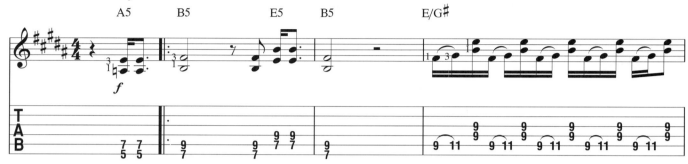

Strum Pattern: 1
Pick Pattern: 5

Intro

Moderately

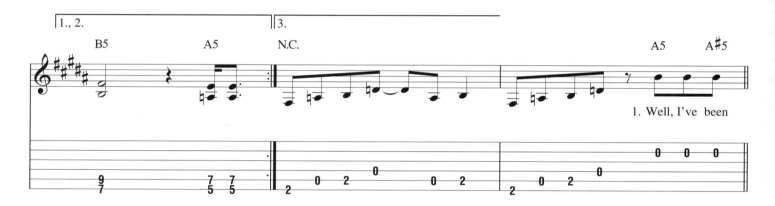

1. Well, I've been

% Verse

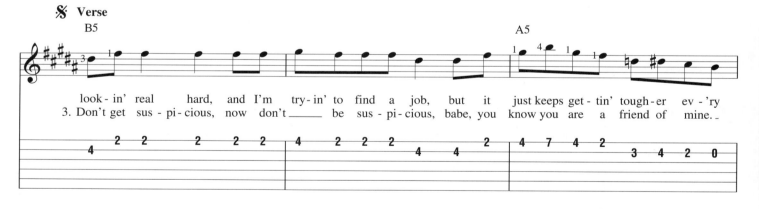

look - in' real   hard, and I'm try - in' to find a job, but it   just keeps get - tin' tough - er ev - 'ry
3. Don't get sus - pi - cious, now don't ___ be sus - pi - cious, babe, you know you are   a   friend of   mine. __

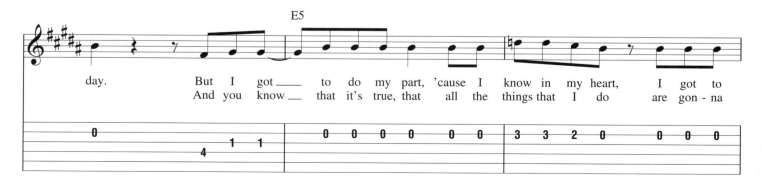

day.   But I   got ___ to do my part, 'cause I   know in my heart,   I got to
              And you know ___ that it's true, that   all   the things that I   do   are gon - na

please my sweet mm, ba - by, yeah, ___ Well, I ain't ___ sup - er - sti - tious, and I
come back to you in your sweet time. ___ I went from Phoe - nix, Ar - i - zo - na, all the

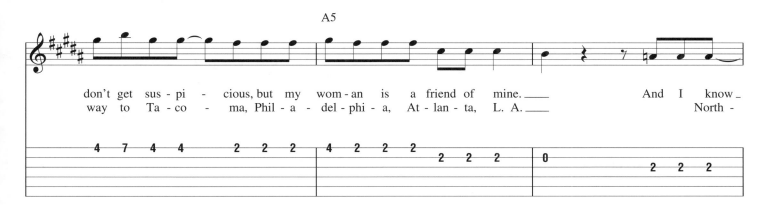

don't get sus - pi - cious, but my wom - an is a friend of mine. ___ And I know ___
way to Ta - co - ma, Phil - a - del - phi - a, At - lan - ta, L. A. ___ North -

___ that it's true, ___ that all the things that I do will come back ___ to me in my sweet - n
- ern Cal - i - for - nia where the girls ___ are warm, so I could hear my sweet, mm, ba - by say. ___

To Coda ⊕

Chorus

B5

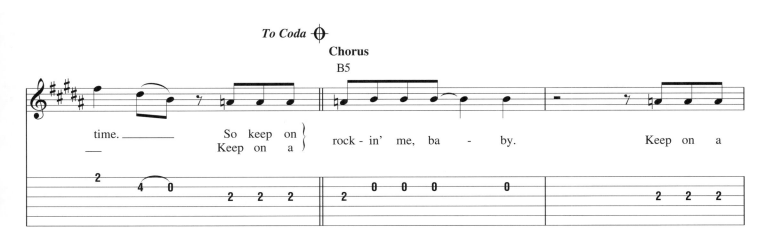

time. ___ So keep on ⎫ rock - in' me, ba - by. Keep on a
___ Keep on a ⎬

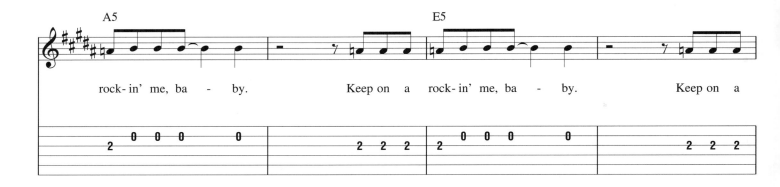

rock-in' me, ba — by. Keep on a rock-in' me, ba — by. Keep on a

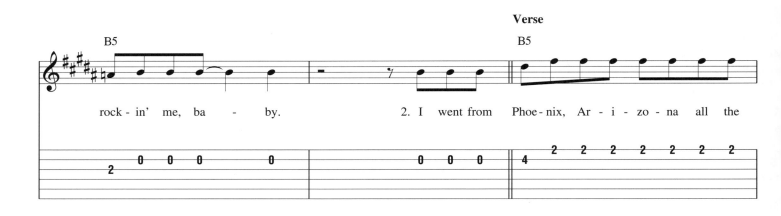

Verse

rock-in' me, ba — by. 2. I went from Phoe-nix, Ar-i-zo-na all the

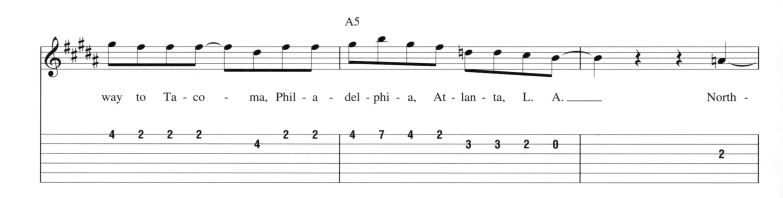

way to Ta-co — ma, Phil-a-del-phi-a, At-lan-ta, L. A._____ North-

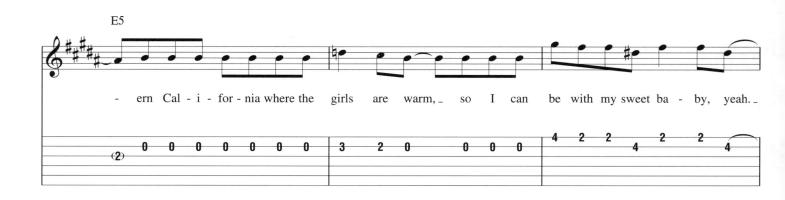

—ern Cal-i-for-nia where the girls are warm,_ so I can be with my sweet ba-by, yeah._

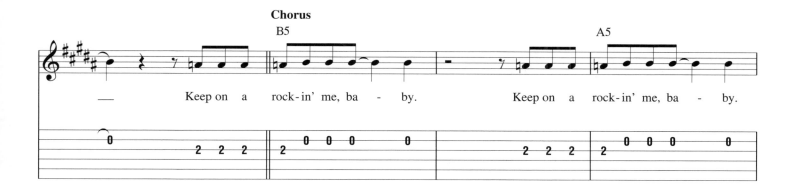

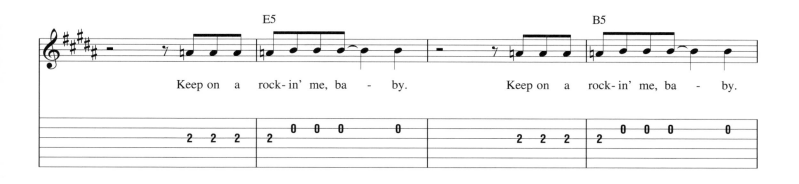

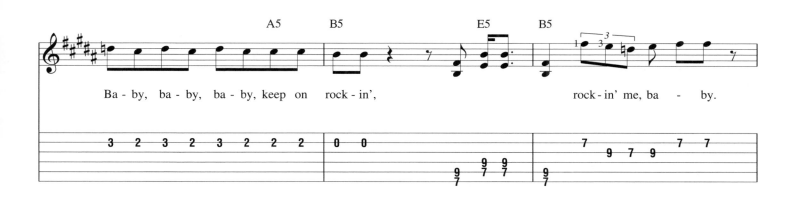

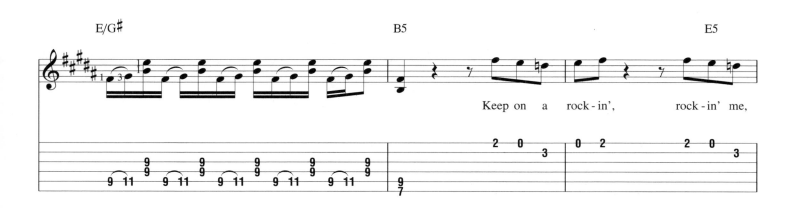

baby.   (Who — who,   who, —

Coda

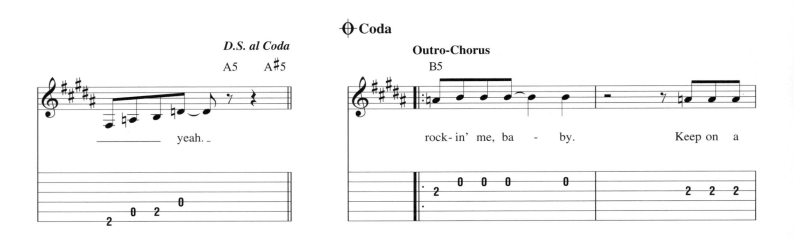

D.S. al Coda

_____ yeah. —

Outro-Chorus

rock-in' me, ba — by.   Keep on a

rock-in' me, ba — by.   Keep on a   rock-in' me, ba — by.

Repeat and fade

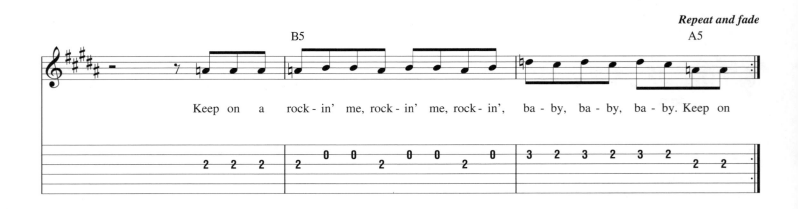

Keep on a   rock-in' me, rock-in' me, rock-in',   ba-by, ba-by, ba-by. Keep on